A Resident's Guide to Madison, Wisconsin

An Anthology of Essays Written by the
Leaders of Madison's Most Well-Respected
Businesses, Clubs, Organizations, and
Events

2017

Table of Contents

About This Series

❖

Wⁿhat is there to do in my city? It's a question we've asked ourselves far too often. It is a natural human tendency to think the grass is greener on the other side of the fence, that we'd have plenty to do if only we moved to another city. The problem with this sentiment is that it ignores the plethora of distinct opportunities and means of exploration that are unique to each American city—from the metropolises of the coasts, to the farming towns of the Midwest, to the mountain villages of Alaska. Seek, and you will find ample opportunity for fun, for immersion, and for growth.

In this series, Z Publishing House gives the leaders of various cities' most respected businesses, shops, organizations, non-profits, and events the chance to tell their own personal story; why they do what they do, sell what they sell, and help who they help. The authenticity of these essays gives an inside look into the humanity behind each of these establishments, as well as their uniqueness, so that you'll never have to ask what there is to do in your city again!

Madison—A Very Special Place
March Schweitzer

Have you noticed that Madison seems to be on the short list of almost every organization that puts out "a best of" list? Voted one of the ten happiest cities in the world (yes, really), best college football town, best farmers' market, best place to retire and best city for young adults, for young entrepreneurs, for quality of life, for biking, for green living, you name it: Madison's on it. While we all know that we should take these lists with a grain of salt, the sheer consistency of these listings leads one to ask the question, why Madison?

Many of the things to do in Madison will point out all the yummy, fascinating, cool, and frequently free stuff you can do when you get here. My focus is on Madison itself. Back in the 1850's, Horace Greeley, editor of the *New York Tribune*, came through and wrote that "Madison has the most magnificent site of any inland town I ever saw." And he wasn't the first to take notice of its beauty. The Woodland Indians saw Madison as a sacred place and built some 1,200 effigy mounds all around the five lakes that form the region. Today, Madison has preserved three hundred of them.

Situated between two large and beautiful lakes on an isthmus that is only ¾ of a mile across at its narrowest point, Madison's downtown is strikingly beautiful and compact. It looks like a much bigger city than its population of 290,000 (including 45,000 students) would seem to indicate. In its center at the highest point is, arguably, one of the three most spectacular capitols in the country. Running nearly four miles along the banks of the largest of the three lakes is the University of Wisconsin. On the shores of the second largest lake lies Monona Terrace, our Frank Lloyd Wright designed Convention Center. And on the smallest of the lakes in the city limits sits the UW Arboretum and Vilas Zoo.

And what makes the city site even more spectacular is that it isn't flat! The terminal glacier that carved out the lakes left drumlins and moraines as it retreated that helped to create a surprisingly steep and hilly landscape and left us with beautifully scenic views.

Then there are the people. Madison has been much loved by succeeding generations of citizens, and it shows. Philanthropy has been a common thread almost since the city's founding in 1837 and has resulted in community projects such as our amazing park system and the Overture Center of Performing Arts. Madisonians care passionately about their city and each other. The civic culture is robust, volunteerism is huge, and there is a palpable sense of purpose to make the city the best it can be. Oh, we have our problems—every city does—but here, there is a drive to make it a great place for all to live.

Museums

UW Space Place
James Lattis

UW Space Place is the outreach and public education center of the Department of Astronomy of the University of Wisconsin-Madison. Since 1990, UW Space Place has offered a broad range of programs, workshops, exhibits, and astronomical events for schools and the general public. All public events are free. There is a fee for group visits, which are by appointment only.

Regularly scheduled programs include guest speakers on astronomical topics (second Tuesday of each month, 7:00 p.m.), monthly programs about current sky events (third Friday of each month, 7:00 p.m. CST or 8:00 p.m. CDT), and science programs for families at 10:00 a.m. every Saturday during the school year, except for holidays.

UW Space Place is located at 2300 S. Park St. in south Madison, inside the Atrium of the Village on Park. This is some distance away from the main UW campus, which allows us to provide plenty of parking and easy access for the community. Space Place extends into the community in many ways too, including frequent programs at schools, libraries, summer camps, and the like. Space Place also created Planet Trek Dane County, a scale model solar system accessible by foot or bicycle that stretches along local recreational trails.

The astronomers of the University of Wisconsin have been dedicated to public outreach since the earliest days of their research on the campus, when Washburn Observatory was first opened to the public in 1881. This dedication to sharing the exploration of the universe has only deepened since UW astronomers began building the scientific instruments of the first space observatory: the Orbiting Astronomical Observatory 2, which was the direct predecessor to the Hubble Space Telescope. Owing to the success of OAO-2 created by the UW Space Astronomy Laboratory (a division of the Astronomy Department), NASA awarded major contracts for instruments to fly in the Hubble Space Telescope as well as aboard Space Shuttle scientific payloads. UW astronomers also pioneered high energy astronomical observations, building instruments for gamma-ray, and especially x-ray, observations from space-based instruments. Space Place extends a long tradition of astronomy outreach into space science.

UW Space Place's permanent exhibits feature several of these major instruments that have been returned from their missions in space, including one of the primary science instruments from the Hubble Space Telescope, which was removed and returned to Earth on the first servicing mission. Other permanent exhibits cover IceCube (UW-Madison's neutrino telescope, which operates in the South Pole) and Wisconsin's large optical telescopes (which operate in Arizona and South Africa). Other exhibits explain astronomical research topics such as the structure of galaxies and the applications of the electromagnetic spectrum. UW's expertise in modern astronomy grew out of the hard-won mastery of a technique called photoelectric photometry, which UW astronomers created and employed with spectacular results beginning in 1922. Our historical exhibit traces UW's astronomical work from the earliest days through the era of space astronomy.

UW Space Place is one of the many efforts that the University of Wisconsin-Madison extends to leverage its research and teaching missions for their mutual benefit and that of the public. From helping kids build their first telescopes and showing where to point into the sky, to describing how to build a space-based instrument or a neutrino telescope, Space Place honors and advances that investment in mankind's knowledge of the universe created and sustained by the people of Wisconsin.

Frank Lloyd Wright's Unitarian Meeting House—First Unitarian Society
March Schweitzer

There are few places in the world that can boast more than a couple of Frank Lloyd Wright designed buildings. Madison has ten of them. Why so many? Wright's family moved to Madison in 1878 when he was ten, and they lived there until Wright moved to Chicago in 1887 to seek fame and fortune. Also, Madison was the closest big city to Spring Green where Wright lived for the last sixty years of his life, and it served as his major commercial, financial, and transportation center during that time. Wright had many ties to Madison and made many friends, and enemies, here.

While most of Madison's Wright structures are private residences (including Wright's first Usonian home, Jacob 1), the most significant among Wright's public buildings is the Unitarian Meeting House, a National Historic Landmark. The Meeting House was designed in 1947 and completed in 1951. The design quickly had a profound impact on ecclesiastical architecture in the United States and beyond. Before the Meeting House was built, church architecture consisted of rectangular boxes with steeples. Wright's decision to meld the steeple and auditorium into a soaring, triangular space was revolutionary for its time. Wright was a third-generation

Unitarian and the unique triangular design is a metaphor for aspiration, which was his understanding of what Unitarianism is about.

Because of its importance, the Unitarian Meeting House has been designated as one of the seventeen most iconic Wright's works by the American Institute of Architects. We also know the building was a favorite of Wright's, as it is graced with the official Frank Lloyd Wright seal of approval—a Cherokee red tile embedded in the wall by the entrance, one of only 50 of his buildings to be so honored by the architect. The history of the construction of the building is the stuff of legend. Cost overruns on this "country church" were huge and nearly bankrupted the 150-member congregation as well as the building's long-suffering contractor. Members of the church hauled one thousand tons of dolomite from a quarry about thirty miles away to save money, and some craftsmen, as well as Wright's apprentices, donated their time to get the building finished.

The Unitarian Meeting House continues to serve as a vibrant and very active Unitarian Universalist congregation. Tours of the building are generally available at 10:30 a.m. and 2:30 p.m. on weekdays between May and the end of September, and after services on Sundays year-round. The building is closed to visitors on Saturdays and public holidays. Visitors must be escorted and those visiting during other times are only allowed a peek at the Landmark Auditorium. While visiting the church, take time to appreciate the 2009 Leadership in Energy and Environmental Design (LEED) gold addition on the south side of the campus. The sustainable design sensitively interprets Usonian architecture in a 21st century context and is winning awards in its own right. An up-to-date events calendar and tour information are available on our website, www.fusmadison.org/welcome/meeting-house.

Washburn Observatory
James Lattis

Washburn Observatory, of the University of Wisconsin-Madison, has presided over Observatory Hill since construction began in 1878. Almost continuously since the spring of 1881 to the present day, visitors have been welcomed on the first and third Wednesday evenings each month (weather permitting) to observe celestial objects with the 15.6-inch telescope. In the summer, June through August, the observatory opens to the public every Wednesday night after dark, weather permitting. The basement level of the observatory building contains historical exhibits that visitors can view on these public nights. The entire grounds are accessible from the Observatory Drive overlook.

The observatory was a gift from Governor Cadwallader C. Washburn (1818–1882), who built the building and purchased the telescopes, then presented it all as a gift to the State of Wisconsin. Washburn was very wealthy as a result of his businesses, especially his flour milling enterprise based in Minneapolis, which later became General Mills. Washburn's ambition was to equip the university with an astronomical research facility that would be on a par with the Harvard Observatory. In coordination with Washburn's gift, the state legislature appropriated an annual budget for staff and operating costs.

As the first observatory director, the university hired the famous astronomer, Professor James Watson. Watson, who arrived in 1878 as construction was beginning, was very influential in Washburn's project, adding, at his own expense, two ancillary observatories—one for students and another for solar observations. Watson did not live to see it completed, but the Washburn Observatory complex eventually comprised five telescopes and four buildings on Observatory Hill. All that remain today are the main observatory building, housing the 15.6-inch refractor, and the former director's residence, which now houses the La Follette School of Public Affairs.

Most of Watson's successors followed the pattern he set on innovation in astronomical instrumentation. Preeminent among them was Professor Joel Stebbins, director from 1922 to 1948, who was the key agent responsible for the development of photoelectric photometry as a practical technology for astronomers. He also developed it into an established technique, trained new generations of astronomers to use it, introduced it to other observatories, and produced important scientific results with it. Washburn Observatory was the development laboratory, test bed, and scientific headquarters for that new and vital tool of astrophysics.

Washburn Observatory ceased to be a research observatory in 1958, when it was supplanted by a new observatory far from the UW campus. However, Wisconsin's astronomers maintained the technological edge developed in the first half of the 20th century and carried it into the Space Age as they developed instruments, descendants of Stebbins's photometers, that flew in successive generations of astronomical aircraft and spacecraft launched by NASA. Washburn Observatory, with its major contributions to our knowledge of the universe and ourselves, exemplifies the vital importance of public investment in science and the progressive heritage of the people of Wisconsin.

Nathaniel & Harriet Dean House
Ann Waidelich

The Historic Blooming Grove Historical Society maintains the 1856 Nathaniel and Harriet Dean House, 4718 Monona Drive, Madison, WI, as an eight-room Victorian house museum. Furnishings reflect the life of a gentleman farmer and his family during the last half of the 19th century.

As you drive north from Madison's South Beltline on Monona Drive—County Road BB—with the Monona Golf Course on your right, you find a Wisconsin Historical Society marker in front of a cream brick, two-story Italianate house with a porch across the front. The marker tells you about the Dean House and its builder. A brass plaque on the house tells you that it was designated as a Madison Landmark on July 4, 1976, and is listed on the National Register of Historic Places. If you arrive in the afternoon of the second Sunday of May through October or during a special event, you will be invited on a guided tour that will let you step back into the past.

Nathaniel Dean had been a merchant in Michigan before coming to Madison, Wisconsin in 1842 and establishing a dry goods store on King Street. He is known to have bought land in Blooming Grove as early as 1846. By 1880, his five hundred acre farm was one of three big dairy farms in the township, producing wheat, corn, and barley, and supporting 93 milk cows, 11 cattle, and 12 pigs.

In 1847, Nathaniel married Harriet Morrison, who was born in Wisconsin in 1829. They had one son who died in infancy. The Deans lived in the farmhouse for about 15 years before moving back to Madison. This site symbolizes Blooming Grove's early economic and social ties with the City of Madison that bordered and later absorbed much of the property.

After Nathaniel's death in 1880, the house was used by farm tenants for about fifty years until, in 1928, the city of Madison created a golf course and put the house to use as its club house. During Madison's 50-year tenure, the house was left unheated in the winter, floors were damaged by golfers' shoes, and plaster began falling from the walls and ceilings.

In 1971, the deteriorating clubhouse was scheduled for demolition. A group of local residents watched in dismay as other historic properties along Monona Drive were razed. Realizing that some memory of the first settlers ought to be preserved and that the Dean House property was already in public hands, the group had the house inspected for basic stability, and persuaded the City of Madison to rent it to them for $1 a year in return for care and restoration.

Thousands of hours of volunteer labor and more hours of fund-raising have been supplemented by many donations of period furnishings. Today, the summer series of Back Porch Concerts, membership dues, and donations provide the funds to maintain the house as a cultural asset. For more information, visit www.bloominggrovehistory.org, or contact the Dean House via phone (608-249-7920) or email (hbghs@tds.net).

Wisconsin Science Museum
Arianna Murphy

Can you name the hometown boy who finished high school in
Madison, Wisconsin when he was 15, graduated from the
University of Wisconsin, then went on to win not one, but two
Nobel Prizes in Physics, something no one else has ever
accomplished? I often pose this question to people in Madison
as a way of introducing the Wisconsin Science Museum. Only
very rarely does someone correctly identify John Bardeen, the
co-discoverer of the transistor that transformed the electronics
industry, allowing miniaturization and ushering in the age of
the microchip, the computer, and the cellular phone. He
shared the Nobel Prize in Physics in 1956 for this discovery. In
1972, he won his second Nobel Prize for his role in explaining
superconductivity at very low temperatures.

The fact that so few Madisonians know about these
achievements of their native son is typical. We do not honor, or
even remember, the discoveries in science and technology that
have shaped our daily lives, but rather we take them for
granted. The Wisconsin Science Museum was created in 2015
to celebrate and explain the work of scientists, engineers, and
mathematicians who trained or worked in Wisconsin and made
important contributions in their own field of studies. Among
their achievements are the discovery of vitamins (in 1913), the
treatments or cures for rickets (in 1923), anemia (in 1930),
phenylketonuria (PKU, in 1934), pellagra (in 1938), and goiter

(in 1939). Wisconsin scientists led in the development of gene mapping (Joshua Lederberg), achieved the first laboratory synthesis of a gene (Gobind Khorana), and discovered the mechanism of infection by viruses in the class that includes HIV (Howard Temin). Each of these scientists won Nobel Prizes for their groundbreaking work. These people, and many others, are featured in the museum's Hall of Fame.

Scientific research often yields results that are visually striking, and scientific ideas are sometimes most effectively conveyed through artistic representations. The Wisconsin Museum of Science therefore has exhibits that combine art and science to help our visitors understand the science and enjoy the experience. We hope you will come and share this experience with us!

Outdoors

University Ridge
Mike Gaspard

Starting out in the golf business almost 20 years ago in Phoenix, Arizona, people used to ask: "Why should I play at the golf course you work at?" My response is always the friendly customer service or impeccable course conditions or fantastic value. The problem I had with this answer was that there were multiple golf courses in the vicinity boasting the same offer. There was no strong branding and no major differentiation between products.

I can honestly say that University Ridge has something unique. We are the University of Wisconsin Golf Course! Nobody else can say that. From the moment you walk into the golf shop, you are surrounded by and reminded of the Badger brand. Our apparel and golf shop is dominated by the colors red, white, and black. The staff primarily consists of UW-Madison students working their way through college. Bucky Badger can be found entertaining the foursomes during many golf events. The popular motion W logo and W crest are present on just about everything. The UW Men's and Women's Golf and Cross Country Teams make their home at University Ridge. If you want a UW-Madison golf experience, then University Ridge is the only choice.

This brand has attracted many high profile events within the state and country. Starting in 2016, University Ridge began a partnership with the PGA Tour, the Steve Stricker

Foundation, and American Family Insurance to host the American Family Insurance Championship. In its first year, this event brought in over 50,000 spectators and raised over $1 million for charity. In addition to this PGA Tour Champions event, University Ridge has hosted many collegiate events, including the 1998 NCAA Women's Championship, four Big Ten Championships, and annual Men's and Women's Badger events. The golf course is also the annual host of the WIAA State Boy's and Girl's Championship since 1994. We are proud to be the one and only University of Wisconsin golf course.

Play Where The Badgers Play! University Ridge!

Hoofer Sailing Club
Mills Botham

Located at the heart of the University of Wisconsin-Madison campus, the Hoofer Sailing Club has been a pillar of student and community life since its establishment in 1931 by Union Director, Porter Butts and Doctor Harold Bradley. One of six clubs under the umbrella of the Hoofers, the Sailing Club operates out of a beautiful facility on the south side of Lake Mendota, and caters to UW students, staff, faculty, and general community members. Memberships are available on a monthly, seasonal, or yearly basis for very reasonable rates.

The Hoofer Sailing Club is home to the largest inland fleet of sailboats in the country, including small, single-person boats, large cruising vessels, and everything in between. The Sailing Club also hosts an excellent windsurfing program, in addition to a dedicated group of kite-boarders. Other aspects of the club include a renowned youth sailing program, introducing children as young as ten to the joys of sailing, along with developing accessible sailing programs tailored to the needs of individuals with a wide variety of disabilities.

The social dynamic of the club is a longstanding and cherished tradition, and the community amongst our members is tight-knit and well loved. Pirates' Day and Commodores Cup, sailing adventures with a focus on socializing between members, are two annual events amongst others spread out over the course of the season.

The Sailing Club is also home to the Wisconsin Sailing Team, a collegiate racing team, which has garnered esteem as one of the finest in the Midwest and a strong contender at the national level. Over many generations of sailors, the team has produced leaders in the sailing industry, distinguished UW Alum, and even a handful of U.S. Olympic sailors.

The members of the Hoofer Sailing Club are united by a universal love of sailing and spending time on Lake Mendota. Now entering its 86th year, the Sailing Club is looking to its future. Currently in the midst of a massive fundraising project, the club has set plans in motion to build an entirely new, state of the art marina/pier system within the next three years.

Now 1,200 members strong, the Hoofer Sailing Club continues to grow and serve Madison as its premier sailing facility.

Aldo Leopold Nature Center

Nature. It's amazing, especially for the overwhelmingly positive effects it has on people, right? Whether big or small, young or old, rich or poor, nature doesn't discriminate—it affects everyone. From lightening moods and decreasing stress to improving our outlook and overall health, the benefits are endless. How do we know this? Well, because at Aldo Leopold Nature Center, we see it firsthand—we witness nature in action every single day.

First, we see it in the Wonder Bugs as they explore and experience nature for the first time with their parents, fearlessly running into the prairie or curiously grabbing for the skins and skulls on the touch table, beyond excited for the endless possibilities they have yet to discover.

We hear it in the squeals of delight as summer campers release the Monarch butterflies they watched hatch from eggs, grow as caterpillars munching on milkweed, and emerge from their chrysalis' to pollinate the prairie.

We see it in the school groups that visit, too. We saw it in Maria, a shy elementary school student on a field trip, who was reluctant to step off the bus, as she gave a fearless presentation on how trees breathe, reciting all the details from memory just four short hours later.

We've witnessed it as we've watched children grow attending our summer camps, vacation days, and other programs, developing strong relationships with the land and nature, becoming volunteers in our Junior Naturalist program and then going on to pursue degrees in environmental education, biology, and other fields.

But it isn't just the children. We see nature's effects on the families who visit us too, bonding while spotting the first Sandhill cranes of the season on a spring hike or learning about Maple syruping or another seasonal activity at one of our many public programs throughout the year.

We see it in our partners and volunteers, our community members who have developed strong relationships with the land, caring for both it and our mission, encouraging us to continue to fulfill it with their countless commitments year after year.

The point is this: whether we are leading a group of elementary school students on their last field trip of the year, taking a group of summer campers canoeing down the Kickapoo River, or simply preserving the space, welcoming visitors and families to explore our trails, the positive effects of nature on people are countless and we invite you to find your connection with nature today!

For more information about our programs and facilities or to learn how you can get involved, please contact the Aldo Leopold Nature Center (608-221-0404) or visit us online at www.aldoleopoldnaturecenter.org.

Golf Madison Parks
Ryan Brinza

One of the greatest things to do in Madison, Wisconsin, is to just be outside. Whether you enjoy hiking, biking, swimming, golfing, or daydreaming with the sun in your eyes, there is something for everyone to do outdoors in this great city. Playing golf is one of the favorite pastimes of Madison residents as evidenced by the wide array of golf courses that have popped up over the past 20 years. Madison and its immediate suburbs are host to nearly 20 golf courses, but there are four within Madison proper that are rich with history, continue to flourish, are open and accessible for everyone, and are the true gems of the Madison golfing experience.

Glenway Golf Course is the City of Madison's oldest course, built in 1927. This short nine-hole golf course sits closest to the University of Wisconsin campus and is a neighborhood favorite, as well as the golfing destination for students at the UW, MATC, and Edgewood College. It is the perfect course for beginner golfers as well, since it's not too long, not too short, but just right. On many days, you will find the future generations of golfers playing at Glenway through The First Tee of South Central Wisconsin's junior golf program.

Monona Golf Course is a regulation nine-hole golf course that sits on Madison's near east side. Originally, Monona was built as an 18-hole golf course, though as time went on, the

East side of Madison was in need of a high school and so Madison LaFollette was built on the land that made up Monona's back nine. Monona is the home course for The First Tee of South Central Wisconsin as most of their programming takes place in this neighborly setting. Monona itself is a very unique track within the Golf Madison Parks system. It is almost entirely surrounded by Monona rather than Madison, though it is in fact on the Madison's land. The neighborhood views it as a tremendous asset and a favorite after-work hangout.

Odana Hills Golf Course, the "Gem of the City of Madison" as it has been called, was opened for business in 1957 and is easily the most popular golf course in South Central Wisconsin. It sits in a perfect location on Madison's near west side, minutes away from just about anywhere in Madison. After ten years of being open for business, world renowned golfers, Jack Nicklaus, Arnold Palmer, and Gary Player held an exhibition match at Odana Hills with the winner taking home a $10,000 prize. Legend has it that on the picturesque seventh hole, now the sixteenth hole, Arnold Palmer blew his drive nearly 340 yards off the tee and landed behind a big rock that was placed on the middle left part of the fairway. To this day, the rock now nestled subtly in the woods near its original resting place is known as "Arnie's Rock."

Yahara Hills Golf Course, which will celebrate its 50th anniversary in 2018, sits on the far east side of Madison. It was home to the very first United States Women's Amateur Public Links Championship in 1977, which hosted 686 women golfers. This 36-hole facility plays host to many city, state, and regional championships every year. The newly remodeled clubhouse and upgraded amenities are sure to please any golfer looking for a day filled with fun and relaxation. With the choice of two separate 18-hole golf courses on property, Yahara Hills is the perfect outing and event destination in Madison.

If you are looking for accessible, affordable, fun, or challenging golf, the City of Madison Golf Courses will not disappoint. If you live in Madison, you will know that there is a City of Madison Golf Course within about ten minutes from where you live. If you are from outside of Madison, be sure to stop in, say hi, play a round, and enjoy all that Madison has to offer.

Madison Log Rolling
Shana Verstegen & Olivia Judd

When many people think of lumberjacks, they think of burly, bearded, axe-wielding men, but did you know that there are water sports that stem from the lumberjack tradition as well? Log rolling is the art of standing on a spinning, floating log, using speed and direction changes to knock your competitor off the other end without touching them or crossing the center line. We've taught log rolling to people of all stripes for over ten years—beards not required.

During the 19th century, logging reshaped the landscape of Wisconsin and provided a livelihood for thousands of workers. The bravest of these lumberjacks, known as "log drivers" or "river pigs," rode and drove the timber from the woods to the sawmills using the river's current. At the end of the log drives, lumberjacks would compete to see who was the best "birler," or as we call them now, log roller.

The sport has evolved into a serious athletic event featured on ESPN, Outdoor Life, ABC Wide World of Sports, and much more. Men and women of all ages log roll in pools, lakes, ponds, and tanks all over the U.S. and Canada. Each June, spectators gather in Wingra Park to watch competitors from all over the region compete in the Midwest Log Rolling Championships, which is a fundraiser for the Huntington's Disease Society of America.

When we aren't training for competitions, Madison Log Rolling coaches stay busy hosting birthday parties, camp excursions, competitive leagues, and weekly classes. Since the founding of Madison Log Rolling in 2005, the program has grown from two logs and a dozen students to training hundreds of students each year. Our Lake Wingra program now has 13 coaches on staff and over 12 practice logs. Every summer, we welcome hundreds of people to try this unique sport on beautiful Lake Wingra. At first, there is a lot of falling in (but we promise even that is fun!) and over time, rollers get to watch their personal records climb, and eventually begin competing against each other.

We work hard in our classes, but also emphasize enjoying the experience and building community. Team members frequently form friendships that extend outside of class, and it is not uncommon for log rollers to show up in elaborate costumes for our annual end-of-season party. We often hear rollers comment on how "addictive" the sport is, and at the end of nearly every class someone asks for "just one more turn." Log rolling provides an opportunity to get outside and connect with a midwest tradition in the company of wonderful people. We welcome rollers of all ages and abilities to join in the fun!

Art & Literature

Encore Studio for the Performing Arts
KelsyAnne Schoenhaar

Something was missing. When it came to plays about people with disabilities, something was definitely missing. Yes. A few plays existed, but it was people without disabilities who performed in 98.9 percent of them (a rough estimate). Few theatre companies were holding up a mirror to this significant part of our society. Sure, there have been some historic representations. There have been "special" stories. The heroic. The saccharine. The pitiful. But those weren't the people I knew. First of all, the people I knew weren't any more or less special than I or anyone else was. Sex. Drugs. Happiness. Depression. Abuse. Kindness. All of it! The good, the bad, and the ugly—and virtually no one was telling their stories. Only a scant few theatre companies in our entire country was holding a mirror up to nearly 20% of our society. Talk about underrepresented!

I was lucky enough to be able to combine my careers about 17 years ago when I became the founding Artistic Director for Encore Studio for the Performing Arts. Encore is a unique organization that supports and fosters the talents of actors with varying disabilities, including physical disabilities, cognitive disabilities, and people dealing with mental health issues. We also support many people within the spectrum of autism. This is an area in which I have a particularly strong connection.

Finding connections in this world is often difficult for anyone. As a transgender lesbian living at the edge of the autistic spectrum, I have a keen understanding of the complexities and complications this can manifest. Before I came out, I was aware of being on the spectrum (although I didn't call it autism at the time). Me, my parents, my siblings and my children—the genetics are strong. This connection not only helps me to relate to the people I support but I think it also helps the people I support relate to me. With Encore, we've found our natural habitat—or perhaps created it.

Encore is a repertory company that sees the world through a different set of lenses. It's one-of-a-kind and its soul comes from the actors, directors, and playwrights (and what a soul it is). It's my home and where I feel comfortable. Supporting the talents of the people we are fortunate to work with—which include the Encore Studio repertory company, the Encore staff, and the other community actors—is a joy. This is not to say it's easy. We work very hard, all of us, the directors, the coaches, and the actors. And the work we do is important for even the most liberal Madisonian to the most conservative Wisconsinite, both often present at our performances.

Pam (not her real name) is a person with autism and several mental health issues. She was well known in the world she lived in. You could say she was notorious. She said what she thought whenever she thought it. It was sad that many people tended to avoid her if they could. She was one of Encore's first actors and hers was the first story we told. We spent a lot of time one-on-one as I interviewed her and she told me incredible stories—not sweet, not heroic, but compelling and real. And no one in the world could tell them like she did. It was the beginning of something big. Since then, Encore has produced over 50 original pieces and many full-length productions.

I've now been working in the arts for 38 years and nearly 30 years with people with disabilities—17 of which have been at Encore. During that time, I've learned more from the people I support than I have from any professor, any elaborate training, or any supervisor. I learned that people are people. I learned there is little understanding about the lives of people with disabilities. I learned there is little repertoire for actors with disabilities. At 17 years young, there is no question that we have much more to learn and much, much more to share.

Tandem Press
Paula M Panczenko

Tandem Press, at the University of Wisconsin-Madison was founded in 1987, as a self-supporting fine art press and gallery in the heart of Madison. From the beginning, it has been Tandem's intent to bring internationally recognized artists to interact with the students and faculty, and to parallel the overall University of Wisconsin-Madison mission of education, research, and public service— a continuation of the Wisconsin Idea. Since 1987, over 80 internationally renowned artists have visited the Press, including Suzanne Caporael, Chuck Close, Jim Dine, Sam Gilliam, Judy Pfaff, Alison Saar, Mickalene Thomas, and Sean Scully. Over 350 art, art history, and arts administration students have apprenticed at Tandem, and workshops, lectures, and open houses have abounded. The visiting artists have made thousands of prints in collaboration with our master printers and they now hang in museums and corporations throughout the United States, including the Museum of Modern Art and the Whitney Museum of American Art in New York, the Art Institute of Chicago, and the National Museum of American Art in Washington D.C., and the British Museum, just to name a few.

The visiting artists come to Tandem Press because it is an experimental facility. But, Tandem also had an extraordinary influence on the visiting artists. They have the opportunity to explore their creativity, and they can undertake projects which cannot normally be carried out in a commercial facility. Since its inception, Tandem Press has also enabled faculty to work at the Press in formal and informal settings and has provided exhibiting opportunities for them throughout the United States.

The UW-Madison Department of Art has a rich tradition in printmaking, and Tandem Press was created to ensure the university's continued leading role in this heritage. The Chazen Museum of Art serves as the archive for the Press and receives one impression of every print edition.

At least 2,000 members of the community, faculty, and students attend Tandem Programs every year in Madison. Tandem has worked with many departments on campus, including Women's Studies and the American Indian Studies Department. Tandem has also collaborated with Madison's public schools.

Tandem Press (1743 Commercial Avenue) is open to the public from 9:00 a.m. – 5:00 p.m. Monday through Friday and by appointment on Saturdays. We recommend that visitors make appointments with the staff for special tours of the Press. Tandem also co-hosts monthly jazz concerts with the Jazz Studies Program at UW-Madison during the school year.

Bach Dancing & Dynamite Society
Samantha B. Crownover

Chamber music with a bang! Not your mother's Mozart. What would Bach be doing if he was more fun and less dead?

Every summer in Madison, a handful of friends, acquaintances, and professional musicians from all across the country get together as the Bach Dancing & Dynamite Society for a three-week chamber music festival. They converge in June each year to rehearse, eat, laugh, have heart-to-hearts, and present six concerts of traditional and contemporary classical music to an intrepid audience.

Our artistic directors combine their musical ingenuity to create the right mix of repertoire and performers that result in this "serious fun."

To avoid creating a sleepy classical music atmosphere (think stuffed shirts sawing away on their instruments), the musicians tell stories from the stage about the music and its composers as well as their own experience with it. They string together pieces of music by composers such as Clara Schumann, Franz Schubert, and Arthur Foote for concert programs with pun titles like "If the Schu Fits." They give away prizes at the door, like antique silver candlestick holders for their "Silver Jubilee" or even a 50-gallon drum of horse manure for gardening at "Same Carriage Fresh Horses." For intermission features, they host mystery guests like "Nancy Sinatra" singing "These Boots Are Made for Walking," with accompaniment scored for a string quartet, clarinet, and piano (you can guess which program she appeared at!). Every summer, BDDS commissions local artists to create visual art installations that illuminate, punctuate, or float above the music.

The laughing and sighing heard throughout the audience in response to the musicians turns into a deep, personal, and transformative experience for everyone by the time the concert is finished. The mix of music, ranging from delightful confection to thrilling and familiar masterpieces to unjustly forgotten and emotionally wrought works, transforms the casual concertgoer into a seasoned connoisseur by the time the festival is over.

From its home base on the thrust stage in The Playhouse in Madison's Overture Center for the Arts, designed by internationally acclaimed architect César Pelli, BDDS takes its show on the road. Every summer you can also find them performing in the jewel-box historic Stoughton Opera House and Frank Lloyd Wright's National Historic Landmark, the intimate Hillside Theater at Taliesin in Spring Green.

Hipper than an orchestra pit, safer than a mosh pit, we play with fire. You won't want to miss our next season!

Synergy Dance Academy
Kari Fisher

I opened Synergy Dance Academy in the summer of 2012 after being a stay-at-home mom, part-time artist, and community volunteer for thirteen years. Why? Because I knew I could. I had complete faith that a 42-year-old woman with no business experience, no real management experience, and a very anti-math attitude could create a successful studio. Was this arrogant or just naive? Probably a little bit of both but whenever I tried anything new, my dad would simply say *"you can do it"* and I believed him, without a doubt, because he believed in me. My mom did too, of course, but she was a tad more realistic than my dad, who saw me as his little girl who could do no wrong. He still does, and mom is still the one who brings me back to earth by making sure I don't get too big headed, usually by telling me to change my outfit or hairstyle.

My oldest daughter began taking dance lessons at Westside Performing Arts (WSPA) in Madison in 2003 where I soon developed a friendship with the owner and her instructors. In 2010, I started teaching a few classes until April of 2012 when she announced her retirement effective in June. Our dance family was splitting up and hearts were heavy. We understood her retirement as she had been in business for thirty years, but we were still upset about the thought of the teachers and dancers no longer being together. After many discussions with family and friends, in a short amount of time, I decided that the someone who needed to keep these dance teachers and students together should be me. I wholeheartedly believed in the talent these instructors had for teaching dance, from classical ballet to contemporary and everything in between, their individual talents created the complete dancer. Naturally, the name "SYNERGY" was the perfect fit.

I knew I would love being around kids of all ages and I knew I was going to have incredibly hard working dance educators who didn't just teach them steps, but actually *educated* students on the history of movement, choreography, and the dancers who came before them. I knew having a team that could share ideas openly with me and each other would create an environment that would celebrate their passion. I knew that if they were happy, their students would be happy. Happy students equal happy parents and happy parents create successful dance studios. It was just a matter of making it happen—in about eight weeks' time. Luckily, I have a very strong support system consisting of my husband, daughters, parents, and friends who always tell me the truth and encourage me in everything I do. I hit the road running and haven't stopped for five years.

My own dance training came from the Monona Academy of Dance. I took classes in tap, jazz, and ballet for twelve years and was a part of the Wisconsin Dance Ensemble's *Nutcracker* for ten years. I liked dance but it wasn't what I pursued after high school. Instead, I received my degree in Commercial Art and Elementary Education. Marriage and children led to my best job title ever: *Stay-At-Home Mom* to two daughters born in 1999 and 2002. I continued doing freelance artwork as well as mural painting, substitute teaching, and volunteering for various community organizations, including President of the Junior League of Madison, The Ronald McDonald House,

The Madison's Children's Museum, Agrace Hospice Care, Girl Scouts of America, Habitat for Humanity, Leadership Greater Madison, Edgewood Campus School, Fishing Without Boundaries, the Special Olympics, American Family Children's Hospital, and the Susan B. Koman Foundation. Bottom line, I like to be busy, which is good because dance studios are always busy!

Synergy offers classes for ages three to 18 in ballet, pointe, tap, jazz, hip hop, contemporary, and lyrical. But my greatest achievement is our "*Chance to Dance*" program created by my instructor, Sarah Jacobson. "C2D" is a unique class focused on providing children with developmental differences an opportunity to express themselves through music and movement. Using a variety of props, we provide a safe and fun physical class that benefits the child in all areas, from posture to socialization. Sarah's own personal journey with her son who has autism fueled her passion to launch "C2D."

We now have five dance teams, over 200 students, and 17 instructors. I tell my dancers that all they need to do to conquer whatever skill they are working on is tell themselves that they *can* do it and it will happen.

After all, believing in someone is the greatest gift you can give. Thankfully, I get to do that every day.

Midwest Clay Project
Jennifer A. Lapham & Brian Kluge

Midwest Clay Project (MCP) is a community ceramics studio in the heart of Madison's vibrant East Side neighborhood. Founded in 2010 by artist and educator Jennifer A. Lapham, MCP offers a variety of opportunities for adults and children to work in clay, and draws people from the neighborhood as well as the greater Madison region. The fully equipped studio is home to a diverse and welcoming community with members ranging in age from five to 75, some retired, others starting their careers, some who love to dabble and explore, and others who still want to pursue more professional artistic endeavors. Day or night, you are likely to find people bent over potter's wheels, laboring over hand-built constructions on canvas-covered tables, or fastidiously dipping wares into buckets of glaze.

Currently managed by Madison artist Brian Kluge, MCP offers five sessions per year, of 6-week classes for adults on specific techniques that range from learning to use the potter's wheel, to building a variety of sculptural and functional forms using hand building techniques. In addition to 10 potter's wheels, one of which can accommodate a wheelchair, MCP houses a slab roller, an extruder, and a variety of interesting hand tools and press molds. Our pool of highly skilled instructors includes university professors, local and emerging artists and potters, as well as visiting artists.

Some people opt to give the studio a try through a private lesson, either solo or with a group of family or friends, before signing up for a full session. Our private lessons provide the unique opportunity to work closely with an experienced instructor. These private lessons can be valuable for more experienced students and studio members too, as our instructors offer a critical eye and an encouraging tone to this one-on-one instruction. Additionally, our studio space hosts a variety of opportunities for groups, including Girl & Boy Scout troops, school field trips, birthday parties for kids, teens and adults, and corporate team events. We also advise on special projects and develop commissions for local businesses.

MCP maintains an ongoing schedule of outreach activities with non-profit organizations, some of which serve our immigrant and refugee community as well as pre-school aged children and adults with special needs. However, the bulk of our studio activity revolves around providing a dynamic workspace for our studio members. At the time of this publication, MCP accommodates a community of 50+ individual studio members who have access to the facility and space to store their work. The studio provides an all-purpose stoneware clay and a lively palette of custom mixed cone six glazes. Our staff of professional artists load and fire kilns constantly, allowing information to be learned from each firing. Regardless of your level of experience, MCP offers opportunities for you to work in clay and deepen your knowledge and appreciation of ceramics in a fun and supportive atmosphere.

The Vinery
Denny Berkery

Sharing the beauty of art glass in all its forms is the primary goal of The Vinery Stained Glass Studio. Since its beginning in 1983 in the Madison area, The Vinery has created thousands of custom stained glass windows. In addition to this service, repair and restoration have been an integral part of the business since its inception. Working with a client in collaboration to create that special piece of artwork is most rewarding. I feel very fortunate to be able to provide this service and be part of the creative process.

Having the skill set to restore old windows and lampshades makes our studio one of only a few in this area. It is very rewarding to be able to extend the life of an old art treasure. Over the years we have developed the ability and sources to match old glass, a key component in the restoration process.

Another way that we share the beauty of art glass is through our extensive teaching program. Each week, over 100 students take classes at The Vinery. We teach stained glass, fused glass, glass mosaics, and flame working. Except for Beginning Stained Glass, most classes are one-day long, usually lasting for three hours. Most of our classes are evening classes, except for Saturday classes which are conducted during the day. We also have a drop-in fusing and mosaic center where customers can come in anytime during store hours and create with glass. We have specific projects available and each student is given instructions on how to work with the medium they have chosen. Working with art glass can truly be therapeutic and it is a joy to watch my customers and students as they put aside the stresses of life and allow their creative side to take over. It is my dream and good fortune to be able to provide a space for this to occur.

Wisconsin Union Theater: Where the Greats Come to Play
Esty Dinur

Where will you find the Midwest's longest-running concert series? Who has brought artists of color and performers from all over the world way before the terms "diversity" or "multiculturalism" were coined? What beautiful venues still offer some of today's greatest artists as well as tomorrow's stars? Where do artists get on stage and voice their excitement at performing in the same venue their icons played in? What hall has been known for its superior acoustics for the past 78 years?

The answer to all these questions is Wisconsin Union Theater, located at the Memorial Union in the heart of the UW-Madison campus, right on beautiful Lake Mendota. Boasting both the renovated historic Shannon Hall and the all-new Fredric March Play Circle Black Box, the theater's season offers world music, jazz, classical, dance, bluegrass, blues, and more. Here you'll find artists at the apex of their career, up-and-comers, and a little nostalgia and Broadway, too. All are of the highest quality at very reasonable ticket prices.

The Wisconsin Union Theater also offers two free festivals: the Madison World Music Festival in September and the Isthmus Jazz Fest in June. The former brings outstanding artists from all over the world for performances and workshops on the Memorial Union's Terrace, in the theater's venues and elsewhere, the latter presenting local and regional artists on The Terrace.

Unique in the way it is ran, the season is booked by a mix of arts professionals and UW-Madison students who get a unique opportunity to work in the real arts world before ever graduating. Indeed, students are important in all aspects of the theater's functions, working behind the scenes with the technical directors, at the box office, with the communications director, as ushers and front of house personnel.

Students also perform in the theater. From Chinese New Year and India Night to Shakespeare plays to the annual Humorology extravaganza, young people cut their teeth here. They act, sing, dance, create scenery, direct, and more on these professional stages and with the help of seasoned arts professionals.

Looking for some great performances at a reasonable price in a beautiful, comfortable, and friendly venue? The Wisconsin Union Theater is where the greats come to play. You can come as you are and leave transformed!

Health & Fitness

Dance Life Studio and Fitness
Arielle Juliette

Dance is a primal part of the human experience, crossing nearly every cultural and temporal boundary. Sadly, many people feel that dance is inaccessible to them because of how our culture has informed us a dancer needs to move or look. Dance Life began because the owner, Arielle, believes dance is for everyone, and it became her passion to help others find joy, self-esteem, and a positive self-image through movement and a strong dance community.

Arielle took her first belly dance lesson by Mona N'wal with her mom, Kathy, at the age of 17 while going through a very dark time in her life. Consistently stuck in a pattern of emotional and sexual abuse, Arielle felt disconnected from her body and loathed looking in the mirror. Through increasingly regular attendance at classes, Arielle found she was able to reconnect with herself again, and to appreciate her body for all the new skills it was gaining, and all the joy it brought her when she allowed the music to take over.

In 2010, Arielle was offered a wonderful opportunity to open her own studio with her investors, Uri and Lyn Fried, and together they took the plunge on a 5,200-square-foot dance facility on Madison's west side. Since then, with the help of Kathy and the incredibly dedicated team of staff volunteers, Dance Life has been offering the most fun dance and fitness classes and events for adults that you can find in one place. We specialize in belly dance and burlesque techniques, and performance and dance fitness classes like Zumba. You can find a variety of other classes too, like Adult Ballet, Hula Hoop Fitness, and PiYo. Our events like Burlesque Ladies' Nights and Inappropriate Song Night are incomparable! In all our classes, workshops, events, and performances, we encourage wellness, fun, and creativity through movement without making you feel like you need to look, act, be different before you can start enjoying yourself.

Come as you are regardless of size, shape, ability level, age, race, etc. and you will not be judged. We're here to have fun and get into our bodies!

Body Harmony
Jennifer Crye

It feels good and it's good for you! In 2000, I started Body Harmony in a one-room office above a Chinese restaurant. Since then, I have taken on a partner and we now have a group of amazing bodyworkers offering Massage Therapy and Acupuncture.

Almost two decades ago, after years of working in customer service on the phone, I was downsized out of a job. While at first I was worried, I was soon to realize that everything happens for a reason. I got a job managing the office for a chiropractor and that was my first introduction to alternative health care. While working as a chiropractic assistant, I discovered massage therapy and I knew this was my next career. I obtained the necessary training with my focus on neuromuscular therapy, sports massage, and trigger point therapy, and got to work at the same time. Over the years, I have gained invaluable experience working with men and women of all ages treating a myriad of complaints ranging from neck and jaw pain to low back pain, foot pain, and everything in between. I have also added myofascial release to my practice which has been very helpful in relieving the stress and pain of my clients. I also enjoy working with expecting mothers before and after pregnancy.

I could not have found a more rewarding career as there are so many ways to help people with the benefits of massage.

You don't need to be in pain to get a massage. Stress is one of the leading causes of poor health. Stress can contribute to heart disease, diabetes, and depression. Massage therapy has been shown to reduce stress by decreasing heart rate and blood pressure. In our current culture of social media, decreasing our contact with other people and where it is not socially acceptable to be overly affectionate, where there is an implied rule that you do not invade another's personal space, we can become very disconnected. Massage promotes relaxation, a sense of well-being, and satisfies our human need for touch in a safe, nurturing environment.

Both sports athletes and computer athletes alike repetitively use their bodies in a way that stresses the muscles and joints. Massage therapy aids recovery by releasing the muscle fibers and increasing the circulation to allow needed nutrients and oxygen to enter the muscles while ridding them of trapped waste products.

At Body Harmony, we have experienced and licensed professionals practicing a variety of techniques to treat any number of issues. The therapists all have their own unique stories about how they have come to practice massage, but one thing they have in common is their caring and dedication.

Whether you want to relax and de-stress or you need more focused therapy to relieve pain or soreness caused by activity or everyday stress on muscles, massage therapy is the way to go. At Body Harmony, you will feel relaxed just walking in the door to our welcoming reception area where you can comfortably wait for your therapist to take you to a warm and inviting room to receive the therapy that will meet your individual needs.

Come and see for yourself!

Float Madison
Greg Griffin

Ten inches of water and 1,000 pounds of Epsom salt equals infinite benefits for the body, mind, and soul. This saltwater solution is the foundation of float therapy.

Growing up on the standard American diet, combined with non-stop partying in college eventually caused me a personal health crisis. After weeks of doctor visits and trips to the emergency room, I finally asked my doctor if my diet of soda, fast food, and alcohol could be the possible culprits for my severe chest pain. His response of, "No, probably not. We'll set you up for a C.T. scan next week," changed my life. I decided to experiment with dieting, cutting out alcohol and processed foods, and within days, the chest pain I had been experiencing for weeks ended, and the acid-reflux I've experienced since childhood was suddenly gone. My journey into living a healthy life of purpose and helping others began.

In 2011, while in school for nutrition, working in the wellness department of my community grocery co-op, my stress levels were becoming difficult to manage. I discovered float therapy while listening to a podcast, and after hearing about the physical and mental benefits, I drove to the closest float center in the area, Spacetime Tanks in Chicago. That first float changed everything. Emerging from the tank, I felt as if my body and mind hit control+alt+delete and I was in a new, brighter, and stress-free alternate universe.

For the next three years, I made the five hour round-trip every few months to float for that reset of body and mind. And with each float, the benefits seemed to compound. Not only were my stress levels down, but aches and pains from my workouts would subside noticeably quicker after floating, and I was creating a meditation practice. Eventually, growing tired of trying to convince friends to open a float center in my home town of Madison, I decided that I would be the one to provide the revolutionary tool to my community.

When I spoke about floating in 2011, most people hadn't yet heard of it. Now, it's the opposite, where most people have at least heard of it, even if they are unaware of the details. If you haven't heard of float therapy, perhaps you have heard of float tanks or sensory deprivation tanks. At Float Madison, we have float pods and an extra-large float room. The pods are quite large, but the room is great for those with concerns of claustrophobia. They are filled with ten inches of water saturated with 1,000 pounds of Epsom salt so everybody will effortlessly float on the surface. Pressure is taken off your muscles, bones, and joints, which vastly improves your circulation and allows your body to rejuvenate and heal. Research shows that floating reduces your blood pressure and heart rate while also lowering cortisol, the main stress hormone. The temperature in the tank is matched with the skin temperature, so after a few minutes you don't feel the water or the air, and it gives you a feeling of floating in space. There are buttons to control lighting and music, but we recommend shutting them off since removing as much external stimuli as possible may help get you into a meditative state a bit quicker.

Floating has been gaining popularity in the past few years, with major athletes such as the New England Patriots, Seattle Seahawks, Chicago Cubs, Olympians, Crossfit champions and more floating on a regular basis. Many celebrities such as Joe Rogan, Drew Carry, Zac Efron, and Elle Macpherson are catching on too.

At Float Madison, we float UW Badger Football players, cyclists, Ironman athletes, Crossfitters, people with chronic pain such as fibromyalgia and complex regional pain syndrome, pregnant women, meditators, and those with mental health disorders such as anxiety, depression, and posttraumatic stress disorder. But the people we see most often are the average stressed Wisconsin workers looking for the best way to wind down and reset from the stresses of daily life.

With floating becoming mainstream, new scientific research to explain the seemingly infinite benefits is a must. The country's largest private brain research center, The Laureate Institute for Brain Research, in Tulsa, Oklahoma, is leading the world in float research and began studies on floating's effect on mental health conditions in 2015. We are very excited to find out exactly how and why float therapy can have such a profound effect on the body and mind.

Whether you are on a spiritual journey, seeking an athletic edge, or simply looking for the best way to manage stress, we invite you to unwind in our warm and spacious private float rooms and pods, and experience the many benefits floating has to offer. Let it be your time to relax, heal, connect, explore, and grow.

Lighthouse Healing Massage Therapy
Kara Donovan-Guido

Lighthouse Healing Massage Therapy was born out of necessity. Kara needed a more focused opportunity to help people heal outside of the confines of a conventional business like a spa or gym.

She believes that the body has infinite wisdom and has the ability to heal itself. It just needs a little guidance, a little space and time, and an occasional nudge. Kara helps facilitate healing by "nudging" the body through massage and other healing modalities, as needed. Each client is treated as a whole person, not just a sore back or a frozen shoulder, and healing is facilitated for the body, mind, and spirit.

Kara is the founder of Lighthouse Healing. Having graduated in 2002 from the Swedish Institute in New York, she now practices massage and shamanistic healing in Madison, WI. Kara is also a Certified Infant Massage Instructor, having studied with the International Loving Touch Foundation. She is a member of the Associated Bodywork & Massage Professionals organization. She currently studies shamanism and has studied herbalism as well.

Kara is a former instructor in the Therapeutic Massage Therapy programs at Globe University in Middleton, and

MATC in Madison. She also teaches infant massage classes to moms and dads!

Kara's interest in massage began in 1999, when her husband became ill with a gastrointestinal condition called Crohn's disease. Instinctively, Kara turned to massage to help him with pain management. Without any formal training, she relied on a healthy dose of intuition, love, and a clear intention to assist with healing. In doing so she found her calling.

Kara continues to work with clients that suffer from chronic health conditions. She also specializes in working with pregnant women and survivors of abuse.

NessAlla Kombucha

In 2008, we founded NessAlla Kombucha in beautiful Madison, Wisconsin, and we've been making craft brewed kombucha using only organic and fair trade ingredients ever since.

Our goal is to promote health and well-being within our community and yours. We came together with the common vision of helping the community gain a deeper knowledge of health and well-being. Both certified herbalists, we began teaching kombucha brewing classes in Madison in 2005. We became well known for our kombucha knowledge and word of our expertise spread. Workshops sold out and we soon had a SCOBY farm growing! We decided to work together to create one of the nation's first small and local kombucha breweries.

We work with a small, dedicated, and totally boochin' team. Our brewery was one of the first craft kombucha producers in the nation, and we're hard at work every day making kombucha, answering questions, and spreading the word through our tastings.

We craft each batch from scratch using our custom blended Rishi teas. For our seasonal blends, we'll add organic and wild crafted herbs that can support your health and well-being. The tea is brewed using reverse osmosis purified water and eco-friendly, on-demand boilers. We currently offer eight regular flavors including blueberry, raspberry, peach blush, juniper rose, lemongrass ginger, mango turmeric, traditional oolong, and a rotating seasonal blend that we change up four times a year depending on the season. We have also started an extensive keg program where we create new flavors that are only available on tap in select locations.

Since we began NessAlla Kombucha in 2008, we've outgrown two spaces and opened a custom built, eco-friendly brewery on the south side of Madison, which we are quickly outgrowing. We've added new flavors, new team members, and new energy, but our commitment to brewing amazing tasting kombucha has not changed a bit. NessAlla is woman owned, has a strong focus on sustainability, and is a 1 Percent for the Planet partner as well as a Green Power leader. We hope you can taste the love.

If you are interested in visiting NessAlla, please sign up for one of our monthly brew tours on our website, www.nessalla.com.

Fun

Old Sugar Distillery
Nathan Greenawalt

Old Sugar Distillery was founded in 2009 by Nathan Greenawalt with the goal of providing unique, delicious spirits to the Madison area. After college, Nathan's passion for craft beverages expanded from beer and wine to spirits. Through his work at a local home brew store, that passion developed into a business plan and Old Sugar was born.

Using local ingredients has always been the priority, and while the original intent of the distillery was to focus just on one or two products, the draw of experimenting with local ingredients resulted in widely varied products. Queen Jennie Sorghum Whiskey is Old Sugar's top seller. It is distilled from 100% Wisconsin sorghum, which is purchased directly from the farmers (accounting for nearly 50% of the farm's sales). The whiskey is smooth and mellow-less sour than a bourbon and less harsh than a rye. Each grain gives the whiskey a unique flavor, and sorghum has proven to be very mild, with the charred oak barrels enriching the flavor.

Old Sugar has managed to expand into brandy production because of the abundance of local fruits. For Brandy Station, a traditional European style brandy, nearly 20,000 pounds of grapes are harvested from a vineyard just 15 minutes south of town. The distillery also makes grappa and a few other brandy variations. In the fall of 2017, Old Sugar is releasing an apple brandy, made from apples grown near Devil's Lake State Park, 40 miles from Madison. Four varietal-specific apple brandies will be released so that customers can see how each apple imparts a unique flavor.

The other flagship products for Old Sugar include Cane & Abe Small-Barrel Rum and Old Sugar Factory Honey Liqueur. Like the whiskey, these spirits are aged in small charred oak barrels, providing notes of caramel and vanilla. The rum is unsweetened and heavily oaked, a rare combination for a rum. It's truly a rum for whiskey drinkers. The honey liqueur is very dry for a liqueur, with just a light sweetness from the addition of local honey. At 80 proof, it's also quite strong for a liqueur, but the goal was to produce a spirit that could stand on its own. It's great either as an after dinner drink or in cocktails. Two of the distillery's most popular cocktails are made with the honey liqueur.

The distillery is open Thursday through Saturday for cocktails and offers free tours and samples to first-time guests. The cocktails feature freshly squeezed juices, house-made syrups, and quality sodas. The Honey-Cap, a cocktail made from muddled lime, local honey, fresh squeezed lime juice, honey liqueur, and soda water has been awarded twice as the best cocktail in Madison by readers of a local paper. It's less sweet than it sounds—along the lines of a margarita or mojito. Although not a restaurant, the snacks available in Old Sugar Distillery are high quality and are made locally. Just a block off the bike path, and with a large outdoor patio, summer is a great time to visit. You can also cozy up next to the warm still on a cold winter night. You can't lose.

Cheers!

The Frequency
Darwin Sampson

I have now lived in Madison for nearly half my life. Never in my wildest dreams did I think I'd be running a small live music venue called The Frequency in a community I love and hope to contribute to as much and as long as possible. The Frequency has afforded me the luxury of keeping music the focus of my life and has provided me years of learning and personal growth along the way. I've met some of my best friends and favorite musicians while witnessing hundreds of incredible shows.

What I really love about The Frequency is the ability to provide a stage and venue of expression in a safe environment to artists from every walk of life. Hosting bands for their first show is one of the greatest feelings I get as a talent buyer and promoter.

While live music is definitely a focus of what we do, we have also hosted a wide variety of events like theatrical productions, comedy shows, even an occasional wedding reception. It's hard to recall every single standout show and act that has graced our small stage in the intimate setting of The Frequency's live music room; I could type a dizzying list of Madison acts alone. National acts such as The Lumineers, Macklemore & James McCartney are some of the bigger names that have treated lucky audiences to an up close and personal experience.

The historic landmark building at 121 W. Main St. is also featured on the route of Madison Ghost Walks. It's true, The Frequency has spirits beyond the alcoholic variety. We have tales of the paranormal, including a physical apparition witnessed by multiple employees. Shaking doors, moving objects, dropping temperatures, and all kinds of fun noises at crazy hours of the night. Good times, great stories.

It'd be more fun if you came in and heard the stories yourself.

ALT Brew
Maureen C. Easton

Come visit ALT Brew at 1808 Wright Street in Madison. Located on the northeast side, a stone's throw from a growing number of great local breweries and beer bars, ALT Brew is Wisconsin's only gluten-free brewery and a 2016 Great American Beer Festival silver medal winner. All of ALT Brew's beers are hand-crafted one barrel at a time in the nanobrewery located onsite. Made entirely of gluten-free ingredients on equipment solely dedicated to gluten-free production, ALT Brew is bringing beer quality and variety back to the gluten-free diet.

Owner and brewer Trevor Easton was inspired to get into gluten-free brewing when his wife, Maureen, was diagnosed with celiac disease and had to adopt a gluten-free diet. As a result, their once shared love of beer—and Trevor's long interest in the brewing process—could no longer be enjoyed together in the same way. At the time, gluten-free options available on the market were limited, many did not hold up to the quality of craft beers, and it was no fun to raise a beer glass alone.

A trained engineer, Trevor sought a solution and developed a gluten-free recipe that lives up to craft beer lovers' expectations. The result? A growing line of craft beers so good you won't know they're gluten-free.

In addition to great craft beer that just happens to be gluten-free, the ALT Brew tap room serves gluten-free food, including charcuterie, Wisconsin artisan cheese, made to order pizzas, and other tasty snacks. ALT Brew also features plenty of entertainment options like tabletop curling, Ms. Pac-Man, and nine pinball machines, including many styles from classics to new releases.

Tours of the brew house are available by appointment or upon request if you happen to see Trevor hanging out in the tap room.

To learn more, visit ALT Brew on Facebook or check out their website. See you at the taproom!

Cat Café Mad
Lauren Glover

When you walk into Cat Café Mad, you'll be greeted at the front by a cat attendant who will explain the rules of the café and introduce all the friendly kitties. Chances are there will be a few cats hanging around the front door, watching people pass in the windows or sitting on the attendant's laps. Once you've gotten your drink (covered to prevent accidents), you can stay up front or wander into the back of the café. The walls are decorated in a forest theme with cat perches imitating the limbs of trees. There are poles covered in carpet on one wall, which the cats love to climb. Comfy leather couches are the favorite lounge spot for many of the cats. There are soft mats on the floor in between them, which are usually covered in cat toys. Lots of boxes and small alcoves are hidden around the couches. There's a set of cubbies against one of the walls, which is a safe area for the cats to retreat to when they don't want to be pet.

On the walls of the hallway leading to the back are pictures and biographies of the cats that call the café their permanent home and the adoptable cats that are looking for a forever home. There are usually 15-20 cats in the café at any time. There are plenty of tables and chairs that are often used for studying or playing the ample supply of board games kept in the café. An attendant can always tell you which cats like to be picked up or what their favorite toys are. There are also cat-themed books to read. Chances are, if you curl up with a good book somewhere, you'll soon have a cat in your lap to keep you company. In the front is a variety of cat-themed merchandise, from cute backpacks with cat ears to calendars with the café cats. The café hosts a lot of events each month from movie showings to knitting circles.

We were inspired to open Cat Café Mad after visiting a cat café in Seoul, South Korea. Cat cafés are a staple of pretty much every city in East Asia. They vary greatly in style, types of cats, and amenities but all follow the same model—you pay to enter and get a drink with entry, are taught the café's rules, and then left to spend time with the cats. There are only a handful of cat cafés in the U.S., and Cat Café Mad is currently the only café in the Midwest. We are also one of the few cafes to have open hours Thursday through Sunday and appointments available all week long.

Cat cafés in Asia often aren't about the well-being of the cats. We wanted to change that for our café. That is why we gave some cats permanent homes, like our special-needs cat, Sebastian, rescued from an abusive situation in Chicago. We have been working with local shelters to find our foster cats' forever homes, even though we're always sorry to see them go! Adoptions have increased 25% for Community Cat Inc., one of our partner shelters. Our café also offers the service of allowing people who can't have cats or are thinking about getting a cat the chance to experience the joys of life with a cat. We often see students coming in around exam time to take advantage of the proven scientific stress relief that a purring cat provides. Overall, we like to think we have made life better for Madison's cats and all the cat lovers out there.

Come visit Cat Café Mad and enjoy a day of cats, coffee, and lots of cuddles.

Forward Theater Company
Scott Haden

In 2009, a national economic downturn, corporate cutbacks, and reductions in foundation giving meant the end for a number of important professional theaters in Wisconsin. This was devastating for the region on many levels: audiences mourned the loss of exceptional productions, theater professionals saw a sharp decline in employment opportunities, and many in the state worried that its "creative class" would relocate permanently.

In response, a group of artists met around a kitchen table to imagine a new professional theater company in Madison: Forward Theater Company. All those gathered agreed that this organization would mount productions that were exciting and meaningful to the audiences of southern Wisconsin. In order to be attuned to the needs of the community, FTC pledged to maintain an active, open, and ongoing dialogue with its supporters, and to employ artists who had chosen to make their homes in the area. FTC has thrived due to its unique organizational structure, its dedication to artistic excellence, its commitment to nurturing regional artists, and its leadership in the community.

FTC has made a name for itself by presenting outstanding productions of extraordinary plays. FTC entertains Wisconsin audiences with Pulitzer Prize and Tony Award-winning dramas, staged readings, new play festivals, world premieres by local playwrights, partnerships with university, professional, and community arts leaders, and Midwest premieres of Broadway plays fresh from their sold-out runs in New York. FTC's bold artistic choices over the course of eight seasons have been rewarded with extraordinary critical reviews and remarkable ticket sales.

By focusing on contemporary, adult theater, FTC fills a needed void in the Madison-area performing arts community. We complement – rather than compete with – other area companies focused on children's, classical, musical, and community theater offerings, thereby contributing to a more complete artistic ecosystem. We select plays that area audiences would not otherwise have an opportunity to see, and have demonstrated our commitment to producing theatrical work by often-underrepresented demographics.

We are committed to strengthening the area's economy by spending locally and employing talented local artists. In 2015-2016, we hired 102 designers, actors, technicians, directors, and stage managers—more than 95% of whom live in Southern Wisconsin. We are particularly proud of our commitment to hiring local artists!

Supporting and developing the talents of Wisconsin's playwrights is also a priority. Since our founding, we have produced festivals of new plays in alternating years with festivals of original monologues. All staged readings and the majority of the monologues came from the pens of Wisconsin writers.

We also strive to create a home for our audiences! Staff, Advisory Company members and Board Directors are present in the lobby before each performance to greet and converse with our audience members. We hold talkbacks with the cast and artistic staff following all of our performances, giving audience members the chance to connect with our artists, and us the chance to learn how our productions are being received.

To make our productions as accessible as possible, we offer reduced-price preview performance tickets ($10, students/educators and $20, general public), discounts for students and seniors, and reduced-price tickets through Overture Center's Club 10 program. At the Playhouse, we offer free pre-show talks before all Thursday and Sunday shows in addition to our post-show talkbacks.

Finally, we partner with other non-profit organizations to enrich our audiences' experience, increase access to our work, and expand the impact of our contemporary and relevant work out to the broader community. We look to organizations that are already actively involved in these issues for guidance on programming that will highlight their needs and give people an opportunity to learn more and get involved.

It's easy to become a member of the Forward Theater family. Just grab a ticket and join us in the Playhouse at Overture Center!

Capital City Food Tours
Brittany Hammer

❖

The love of food is one thing that all humans have in common. And while it is something that we all need to survive, it is different everywhere we go, strongly influenced by the culture and history of a location. When combined together—food, culture, and history—you get a full circle experience of a destination.

Capital City Food tours takes guests on a journey through downtown Madison, creating an emotional connection between the food, restaurants, and the city itself. On the three-hour walking tour, guests stop in to locally owned restaurants to sample signature items while also learning about the owners, how the food is prepared, and the importance of the item in Wisconsin's culture.

The Around the Square Tour features restaurants that are true to Wisconsin, including one of the quintessential brewpubs in the nation that has been acclaimed by many beer publications; a classic family run New York bagel shop that has some of the only hand-rolled bagels in the Midwest, a family-operated fudge shop that uses locally sourced milk and butter; a pre-prohibition style tavern set in a historic building; and a swanky comic book style restaurant that is operated by a local company that is constantly giving back to the surrounding communities.

Throughout the walking experience, guests also learn about the architecture of historical buildings that have been around the Capitol since the 1800's and the businesses that once operated in them during the emergence of Madison. Guests also stop inside Madison's breathtaking Capitol building to appreciate the immense beauty of the building that draws visitors from all over. Here they learn about the men who "discovered" the city and the controversial methods they used to make Madison the capital of Wisconsin. Take a moment to learn about the Dane County Farmer's Market, the largest producer-only market in the nation that people rave about. Then stroll down State Street, the entertainment hub of downtown Madison that constantly has a buzz.

Madison may seem small with only 250,000 people, but it is truly unlike any other city in Wisconsin. The food scene in the city has only continued to grow and evolve with chefs from all over the country choosing Madison as the location to expand their dreams. Capital City Food Tours would love the opportunity to share our home city with you. Whether you are new to Madison or have called this city home for many years, our tour is sure to make you fall in love. Join us on a tour to fill your belly, heart, and mind as we eat our way through Madison together.

Mad-City Water Ski Team
Jacci Meier

Miles of ropes, boats with up to 750 horsepower, sparkly costumes, music, announcing, smiles, and waves can be found at Law Park every Sunday night from Memorial Day to Labor Day. Crowds fill the shoreline of Lake Monona to take in free shows by the Mad-City Water Ski Team that display human pyramids, bare footers, swivelers, jumpers, doubles couples, and much more.

This group of dedicated volunteers not only performs for the Madison community, but also competes in regional and national water ski show tournaments. The team is nationally recognized for its innovative and thrilling shows and they have has won National Championships in 1975, 1976, 1977, 1978, 1979, 2004, 2006, 2007, 2008, and 2009.

During a tournament show, the team has one hour to perform 13 acts and are scored on not only skiing, but everything from boat driving to announcing. In 2016, Mad-City's ballet line had a record 30 girls pulled on their slalom skis off the dock around the show course for two passes, and returned to the beach arm in arm.

A true family sport, the team is made up of skiers from six to 60 years old and a variety of other support personnel. Although there are many people joining the team as individuals, there are also many families that join where parents (and grandparents!) and children all compete on the same team together—some may be skiing and others may be helping on the shore, docks or out in the boats.

Many past and present members have skied professionally at places such as Tommy Bartlett's in the Wisconsin Dells, throughout the world in traveling ski shows in Germany, China, and Japan and at Sea Worlds, Six Flags, and Cypress Gardens. These skilled skiers also hold clinics to introduce new skiers to the sport, many also working with adaptive skiers.

Mad-City is known for a show that holds your attention the entire time, with athleticism on the water and humor and dancing on land. The team practices year-round, retreating indoors in the winter months to practice climbing pyramids four and sometimes five tiers high, and perfecting doubles moves. Members also use this time to sew beautiful costumes by hand, tune up boats, make ropes, and write the show.

If you find yourself in Madison on a Sunday night in summer, make your way to Lake Monona and enjoy the show!

Rockin' Jump Indoor Trampoline & Climbing Park

I was born and raised in the Madison, WI area and spent my first 23 years going to school and living here. I know the area well. It's an amazing place to raise a family, but we also suffer through long winters and hot, humid summers. This is why I moved away shortly after college, seeking new adventures and experiences. Most of that time was spent living in the San Francisco Bay Area. While life there is pretty awesome most of the time (the weather is pretty sweet), every trip home reminded me that I really do come from an awesome part of the country where you can actually afford to buy a home and send kids to public school.

When I was first approached by the four founders of Rockin' Jump in 2010 to create their brand, they had intended to build just one indoor trampoline park in Dublin, CA. Their goal was to build a local brand that put a strong focus on cleanliness, safety, and fun fitness, with engaging staff and an energetic brand approach. The Rockin' Jump name and frog logo was born out of that set of goals, along with this mantra of "fitness and competition disguised as fun." The brand has grown beyond our wildest dreams and now includes over 35 domestic and international locations in early 2017 with another 30 or more in the works.

In 2012, on my annual holiday season visit home to Madison, I realized I was ready to move back. The Bay Area had been awesome, but my friends and family ties were much stronger here than on the West Coast. With my experience with Rockin' Jump, I came back with the intention to build Madison's first indoor trampoline and rock climbing park. Little did I know that a fellow Middleton High School alumnus and his friend were preparing to do the same. It's a longer story than this, but suffice it to say that we came to the mutual conclusion that working together, instead of trying to compete in a smaller market, would yield a better result for all of us. They agreed to join me as Rockin' Jump franchisees and I adopted many of their great ideas for a larger park format than what Rockin' Jump had been building previously.

Our park, when it opened in 2015, was a flagship location for Rockin' Jump. Our custom-built building offers a 55 feet wide and 32-foot high rock climbing wall custom built on location, and our mezzanine and café provided a new template for how concessions and seating or productivity areas for non-jumping adults could be provided. Since opening, we've become Madison's preferred venue for kids' birthday parties as well as the best venue to get a great workout while having an awesome time. Our dynamic party hosts and private party rooms offer a premium experience when compared to other options here in town.

Our attraction space is large, taking up over 20,000 of our combined 28,000-square foot area, and includes a very large open jump arena, an adjoining young children's jump arena, two trampoline dodgeball courts, a trampoline stunt jump air bag attraction, three slam dunk trampoline basketball lanes, a slack line, X-Beam gladiator challenge, and, most recently, the addition of two Sling Shot aerial flipping attractions. As

75

previously mentioned, we have a large mezzanine with multiple TVs and couches, as well as tables for families to rest and enjoy a snack or drink. Our free Wi-Fi and ample seating helps parents remain productive, should they choose not to jump with their kids (yes, a lot of adults jump, too).

We offer a number of specialty jump programs, including:

Rockin' Tot's Time—this is reserved time for kids six years old and younger to jump with children of the same age in a safer, more controlled environment. Parents are expected to accompany their children, but reminded that it is not an adult jump time. We offer Tot's Time Tuesday, and Friday to Sunday mornings. Visit our website for the latest times and pricing.

Rockin' Fridays—this is a later evening jump time party for tweens and teens (11-17 years of age) with a live DJ and our dance club party light system on full display.

Rockin' Saturdays—similar to Rockin' Fridays, this is a later evening jump time party for all ages with a party music vibe and our dance club party light system.

Rockin' Wednesdays—this is our weekly Buy 60 Minutes and Get a Free Upgrade to 120 minutes jump event all day or evening on Wednesdays, and no coupon is required.

We offer a variety of additional specialty discount programs throughout the week in our café, as well as a Frequent Jumper Card that allows you to buy bulk jump time and save nearly 30 percent.

We look forward to hosting you and your family at our park soon.

Wisconsin Union

❖

In Madison, there is no better iconic symbol of summer than the Wisconsin Union's Memorial Union Terrace. This historic gathering place is a quintessential Madison experience and holds a special place in the hearts of millions of people.

What is the Terrace, you ask? It's a shorter list to name all the things the Terrace is not. Among countless other things, it is a concert venue, a gathering spot, a classroom, a dining destination, and an outdoor movie theater.

This expansive outdoor space is right between Lake Mendota, one of the largest lakes in Madison, and the Memorial Union, a treasured place to socialize, relax, study, and be nourished.

While events occur almost daily in the Memorial Union, the warm months on the Terrace, known to many as "Terrace Season", herald in some of the Wisconsin Union's most treasured traditions, such as free films and concerts at night.

Undoubtedly, part of what makes the Terrace so special to so many are the memories made there. The Terrace has been home to friends reuniting, to love stories beginning, to colleagues exchanging ideas, to students learning, and so much more.

Wisconsin Union Emeritus Director Ted Crabb summed up this unique aspect of the Terrace perfectly when he said,

"This is just something special. You sense it in the people who are here and the activity going on."

Together, these events, and the people who attend them, have made the Terrace far more than just a gathering spot during the spring, summer, and early fall. It is a common space where all come together for sunny days, beautiful sunsets, and spectacular nights.

To put it simply, there is an undeniable magic about the Memorial Union Terrace. It has the power to bring together people from all around the world and to join them in their shared experiences for a lifetime.

The Wisconsin Union team invites you to experience the magic of the Terrace for yourself. Visit our website to learn more and to see what experiences of a lifetime await you.

Hemmachef
Chef Joel Olson

Did you know that orange juice comes from inside an orange? Or that creaming butter and sugar doesn't require pouring cream into the bowl, but instead stirring the butter and cream together until they are smooth and creamy? What about sweating vegetables with their own liquid, not yours? These are all questions students in cooking classes have raised! You too can get answers to all of your pressing culinary questions by taking one of Chef Joel's popular cooking classes in Madison.

Whether you want to spend time with your god-child learning how to make pasta, learn how to use that Henkels chef knife that you got as a house-warming gift, prepare fun appetizers that go well with a nice Chardonnay on a Friday evening with friends, or learn how to best filet a Bronzino, Hemmachef offers great cooking classes. Chef Joel's children's classes offer kids not only basic culinary techniques such as knife skills, but also advanced bread-baking skills, techniques to make perfect omelets, and a class dedicated to creating homemade Ramen noodles. Chef Joel will also come to your office or home to offer fantastic in-home cooking parties, professional team-building events, and even children's birthday/ cooking parties. If you and your co-workers can use sharp knives together to prepare food and sit down and eat together, you can definitely get that proposal done as a team!

Chef Joel's quick wit and mid-Western charm make him a popular teacher and presenter, whether he is teaching a small class of eight year olds, presenting to a large audience of culinary professionals, or appearing on television. Through Hemmachef (which means "home chef" in Swedish), Chef Joel offers classes for all ages and levels of skill, for anyone interested in learning to prepare delicious food. He brings his unique flair to culinary instruction, approaching teaching as entertainment and using his sense of humor and passion for cooking to inspire and involve his students. He is adept at working with people and making sure that everyone has a fun culinary experience while learning useful skills.

Chef Joel especially enjoys inspiring people to love cooking and enjoy good food. He specializes in several areas:

Using classic French culinary techniques to prepare all kinds of food—from wild game, to traditional Wisconsin comfort food, to haute cuisine;

Teaching children and empowering them to make good choices about the food they eat and how they eat it, and giving them the skills to prepare delicious food for themselves and others;

Teaching manners and etiquette and why they are important, both in food-related settings and in daily life;

Working with people of all levels of ability, including those with physical and developmental disabilities. He feels strongly that everyone can successfully participate in culinary classes and works hard to ensure that all students fully participate in each class;

Preparing Wild Game. Chef Joel Olson is a proud Wisconsin native and an avid sportsman. He has combined his love of hunting and fishing and his classical culinary training to

80

develop expertise in preparing innovative dishes with Wisconsin fish and game, from squirrel to venison to snapping turtle. He has hosted an annual "Game Feed" in Wisconsin for the past 20 years to share his love of cooking game with friends and family and to showcase different gourmet preparations of wild game and fish.

The World's Largest Brat Fest
Emily Skaer

The World's Largest Brat Fest has been an iconic kick off to summer in Madison every Memorial Day Weekend since 1983, thanks to Tom and Margaret Metcalfe. The first Brat Fest took place in the Metcalfe's Market Hilldale parking lot (Madison, Wis.), as an effort to thank the customers of Tom and Margaret's family-owned grocery store. Brats were cooked up on a Weber grill and sold for 50 cents. People from all over Madison began flocking to the store every Memorial Day weekend.

As time went on and word spread, more and more people filled the Metcalfe's parking lot over Memorial Day weekend and Tom and Margaret realized they needed help. Having strong roots within the community, they decided to donate the brat proceeds to organizations whose members volunteered to help cook and serve the brats.

After selling 35,000 brats on Memorial Day in 1999, Tom asked his brat supplier, Johnsonville, if that was a lot of brats. After some deliberation, they told him they thought Metcalfe's was hosting The World's Largest Brat Fest, and the name was born just like that. After claiming the title, Tom and his two sons, Tim and Kevin, began to count the number of brats sold.

In 2004, they sold a whopping 189,432 brats in the parking lot. At this point, it became evident Brat Fest had outgrown its humble beginnings and needed a new home. In 2005, The

World's Largest Brat Fest moved to Willow Island at the Alliant Energy Center with the hopes of growing this tradition. Willow Island proved to be a great fit for The World's Largest Brat Fest and it was voted "Best Outdoor Festival" by Madison.com readers in 2008, 2009, and 2010.

Brat Fest has since evolved into more than just a food festival. Brat Fest brings the community together each Memorial Day weekend for four days of free, live music, fantastic food, and family-friendly fun in the heart of downtown Madison.

Since its humble beginnings, Brat Festers have consumed over 3.8 million brats to benefit over 100 charities. Brat Fest is a volunteer-run nonprofit event that provides an opportunity to be a part of something that benefits the entire community. With over 3,200 volunteers, the record for money raised in a single weekend is $150,000. Since 1983, Brat Fest has raised over $1.75 million for local charities with no sign of slowing down.

Thanks to Tom and Margaret Metcalfe and their desire to give back to the community, all of the volunteers and the City of Madison's declaration, Madison is now known as the Brat Capital of the World! Since 1983, the number of brats that have been enjoyed is in the millions, including a World Record of 209,376 brats in 2010.

Tania Tandias Flamenco & Spanish Dance
Tania Tandias

I was first introduced to flamenco, an art form native to Spain, through the soul of the music—captivating guitar melodies and passionate song. Flamenco is the product of the Spanish gypsies, a historically oppressed people, and has musical and dance styles ranging from the deeply serious and tragic to the festive and gay. Because of the hardship of gypsy lives, flamenco became an emotional outlet for these passionate people.

As a young person growing up in Madison, who tended to be reserved and somewhat shy, I felt the elemental nature of the music and rhythms reaching out to me. Flamenco dance then became a new and powerful way for me to move and express myself. After a few years of training, I decided to dedicate my life to flamenco and therefore needed to venture outside the borders of Wisconsin to further my education.

My studies took me to places such as San Francisco, Albuquerque and Seville, Spain. After a number of years of study and performance, I felt compelled to return to my home town to be with family and share the beauty of the art form within a state that has relatively little knowledge of flamenco. Since this time I have cultivated a community of flamenco students and aficionados within Madison and now have a company that performs across the state, dancing at venues of all sizes, from schools and festivals to operas and ballets.

Besides presenting my own company or solo performances, I continually strive to bring awareness to this cultural art by offering public performances featuring flamenco artists from the United States and Spain. The majority of my business, Tania Tandias Flamenco & Spanish Dance, is focused on my dance classes, which range from the very basic beginning through intermediate/advanced levels and are made up of students from all backgrounds and ages. Dancers learn to master basic flamenco dance technique, including percussive footwork (zapateado) and handclapping, graceful hand movements, flowers (flores), arm work, and snappy turns. Students are also encouraged to participate in extra enrichment activities like annual student recitals and workshops taught by visiting guest artists.

It is a very fulfilling experience for me to share my love of flamenco with the Madison community and witness how people's lives are touched by finding joy and expression in movement and music. Come visit us and experience for yourself the magic of flamenco through its compelling rhythms, swirling colors, and passionate dance! ¡Olé!

Madison Scottish Country Dancers
Nancy McClements

What is more fun than exercising? What's more social than tango and less stressful than ballet? Scottish Country Dancing! For more than 40 years Madison Scottish Country Dancers (MSCD) have been teaching and enjoying the jigs, reels, and strathspeys of Scotland every Sunday night, and you are invited to join us.

Unlike the showier Highland dancing (fling and sword dance), Scottish Country Dancing emphasizes social interaction. Participants typically dance in sets of six to eight people to lively fiddle, accordion, and piano tunes. Once you learn a few basic steps and formations, you'll be able to do hundreds of dances. Scottish dancing is enjoyed all over the world. No Scottish background is needed, and dancers of all ages are welcome. Our dancers range from age eight to 80! You don't even need a partner to participate because we change partners with every dance. Dance experience is not necessary. We all started off as beginners and we try to make everyone feel welcome. Knowing your right from your left is a good start.

We meet Sundays at the Wil-Mar Neighborhood Center, 953 Jenifer St., on Madison's near east side. Class begins at 7:00 p.m. with basic instruction then continues with progressively more challenging dances until 9:30 p.m. A mid-evening break with tea and cookies allows time for announcements and chatting with fellow dancers. Don't have a kilt? Not a problem! We save the tartans and sporrans for our fancy balls, and on Sunday nights, blue jeans and skirts are more typical. Soft-soled shoes or even socks will work best for your feet. There is no charge for first-time attendees. Classes are taught by a rotation of local teachers who go through rigorous training and are certified by international experts.

Although Madison Scottish Country Dancers dance for personal enjoyment, we also occasionally perform at street fairs, international festivals, and private functions. We hold a formal ball each spring, with live musicians who specialize in Scottish music. In the summer, we combine with the Chicago and Milwaukee Scottish dance groups to offer a weekend workshop with nationally-known teachers and musicians. Our members travel to other countries (or just down Interstate 90) to participate in annual balls and workshops.

Our group is a part of a much larger organization—we are the John Muir (Wisconsin) Branch of the Royal Scottish Country Dance Society (RSCDS) in Edinburgh, Scotland. Because of the oversight of the RSCDS, Scottish Country Dancing is taught and performed with the same standards and dances throughout the world. Although some of the dances originated in the 18th century, new ones are being devised continually, and number in the thousands. We teach the "old favorites" along with 21st century offerings.

It's often difficult to find entertainment on a Sunday night in a new town. If you'd like to watch instead of dance, you're welcome to enjoy from the side lines, but don't be surprised if

you're invited to the dance floor and find yourself reeling
before you know it!

The Currach
Joshua Perkins

Walking off the street into a warm pub or public house (bar or tavern to American ears) and hearing a live session of traditional Irish music is an experience neither rare nor common, but which isn't soon forgotten. You might hear a thumping reel or jig, or one of hundreds of ballads describing the joys and sorrows of home, love, and war. As much as flags, politics, or conversation, music binds the Irish community and all those who find a welcome in it, and a live session distinguishes a true Irish pub from the pretenders. In Madison, The Currach (Irish for canoe, or open boat) has played that role along with playing the reels for over a decade.

For those who haven't heard many live sessions, the band may bring surprises. Yes, a lively fiddle is there, along with songs familiar to all from groups like the Clancy Brothers and The Dubliners. But, the band draws inspiration from many quarters and you are as likely to hear a Scottish whaling song or gentle waltz as you are a rousing paean to the charms of a pint of Guinness. The band is very fond of a song and loves an audience ready to sing along and make requests.

Another surprise for those who are used to formal performances is how the band does not sit or stand on a stage, hidden by microphones and speakers. Like the great musicians and storytellers they learned from, they take a seat nearly amongst other pub goers and the music can only be as loud as acoustic instruments will play. Irish traditional music is not meant to overwhelm conversation or mark a line between listener and player. It is meant to flow between and bind those who are near and listen with affection. The Currach follows this idea to the letter, which is really no more than following the example set by the great players they learned from in Ireland and America.

Recently expanded from a trio to a quartet, the members of the band all came to Irish music from individual journeys and met under the roof of the Brocach Irish Pub in Madison's Capitol Square nearly 11 years ago, each bringing a handful of songs and tunes to combine into a dinnertime session every Friday night. Now, visitors in Madison can see the band each Friday at the Brocach Monroe St. from 6:00-7:00 p.m. and on the second and fourth Sundays of each month at the Capitol Square Brocach from 5:00-6:30 p.m.

Hop Head Tours
Justin Schmitz

The idea of putting together a bus, a group of people and a lineup of breweries to make a tour came to me one day after skiing at my local hill about 30 minutes from Madison. Just a few miles from the ski hill, there is a brewpub named the Grumpy Troll and I wanted to stop and try a sample platter of all their beers. Unfortunately, it wouldn't be wise to drive after all that beer. At that same time, I realized that I try to find local breweries to visit, sample their beer and get a bite to eat whenever I travel. It dawned on me that there must other people who wanted the same thing I did; safe transportation to multiple breweries to sample their beers. With two friends collaborating on the idea as business partners, Hop Head Tours was born!

Hop Head Tours (originally Hop Head Beer Tours) started off in 2010 by renting motor coaches and promoting group travel tours to places likes Chicago, Milwaukee, Central Wisconsin for touring, tasting and learning interesting facts and history along the way. After three years learning how we wanted to operate and market our tours, we decided in 2013 to purchase our first 14 passenger shuttle bus so we could start offering local tours featuring the exploding brewery scene in Madison. We also started to diversify the types of stops we included with wineries, distilleries and other related attractions.

After another three years of itinerary experimentation, great reviews and steady growth, we hit our stride and decided to buy a second bus in 2016. We wanted to offer local tours in Milwaukee featuring the deep German brewing roots of the "Beer Capital of the World" and the craft brewing scene that was just starting to take off. This was a big leap for us, not only financially but also to really double down on our and our staff's knowledge of beer and alcohol history by making history narration on the bus during our local tours an integral part of our experience.

We're still offering group travel tours to areas of Michigan and Chicago and we're about to embark on our first International trip, the Bavarian Beer Tour, in September 2018! It's been a wild ride, a lot of work, sweat and tears but at the end of the day, I get to do what I love most: entertaining people with history stories and educating them about beer!

Shops

Calliope Ice Cream
Staci Fritz

We think of ice cream base as a blank canvas. Although chocolate and vanilla are lovely, there's a whole world of food just waiting to be explored through our medium. Welcome to Calliope Ice Cream in Madison.

Naturally, all our ice cream starts with good Wisconsin dairy and cane sugar. It is considered a super-premium ice cream, with 14% milk fat and a low (~35%) overrun, making it very dense, creamy, and flavorful. But what sets us apart are our flavors.

Being the Dairy State, we have a lot of great ice cream being produced here. But there wasn't any made for adults (or anyone else who was ready to try something just a little different from the ice cream they grew up with). In 2012, Calliope was founded to develop, discover, and explore the awesome flavor combinations that exist outside the traditional ice cream box. Our current line-up includes:

Brandy Old Fashioned—Wisconsin's favorite cocktail turned into a luscious, cherry-forward ice cream. The state's Old Fashioned drinkers are happy with it, and that's all we need.

Crispy Rice Treat—your favorite childhood bake sale treat is now available as chewy chocolate crispies in a marshmallow or vanilla ice cream base.

Graham Cracker—it's the best version of a graham cracker, with all the flavor you love turned into a smooth, cool, creamy ice cream.

Hearty Breakfast—French toast, bacon, and just a touch of Madison's own Queen Jennie Sorghum Whiskey is the ice cream that's been missing from your life.

Hot Peanut Butter—sweet and peanutty with a tiny bit of Sriracha chile paste for kicks; it's a great mash-up of Thai spice and Midwest sensibility.

Lemon Lavender—lavender flowers in a light and refreshing lemon base; this is a perfect dish for summer, or any day you wish was a summer day.

Mexican Hot Chocolate—cinnamon, chocolate, and chipotle pepper…you want to know how ice cream can be hot? This one packs an unforgettable spicy punch.

Food. Love. Fun.

Food. Food sustains us. Not just in the "you have to eat to live" sense, but in the way it shapes our lives, our interactions, and our identities.

Love. If you don't have love, what do you have? Not much. "Not all of us can do great things. But we can do small things with great love."

Fun. Hard work and fun are not mutually exclusive. The things we have to do might feel less like work if we remember to have fun while doing them. You can find Calliope Ice Cream sold by the pint at grocery stores and restaurants around Dane County. It is also available in three gallons for special events—wedding, receptions, graduations, and ice cream super-fans with plenty of freezer space.

Chocolate Shoppe Ice Cream Company

❖

Let's be honest, you can't come to the capital of the Dairy State without stopping at a genuine Wisconsin ice cream shoppe. As a second generation, family owned and operated company that's been making rich, handmade ice cream batch by batch out of Wisconsin cream for over 50 years, Chocolate Shoppe Ice Cream has you covered! With six convenient Madison locations, we offer a variety of ways to satisfy your sweet tooth. Visit our flagship shoppe on downtown's bustling State Street and enjoy a fresh-baked waffle cone with our award-winning Zanzibar® Chocolate, or take a break from your busy day with a scoop of This $@&! Just Got Serious™ (salted caramel, sea salt fudge, cashews) on the outdoor patio of our Atwood walk-up window. We offer treats for the whole family with vegan, gluten-free, and low-sugar options. So, if you find yourself in beautiful Madison, we hope you'll give our award-winning ice cream a try, and remember, if you want nutrition, eat carrots!

Batch Bakehouse
Susan Linley Detering

At Batch Bakehouse, we make bread and pastry the old-fashioned way: before dawn, from scratch, using only the finest ingredients, with each piece carefully crafted by hand. We specialize in croissants and pastries, French baguettes, and artisanal loaf breads. Every day, our pastry chefs fill our case with a wide variety of sweet and savory treats, including croissants, cookies, cakes, pies, tarts, bars, brownies, galettes, biscuits, tea cakes, shortbread stacked sandwich cookies, individual quiche—the list goes on. In the wee hours of the morning, our bakers hand shape loaf breads and roll classic croissant.

Lauren Carter, Owner, Pastry Chef:

Baking since she could reach the counter in her mother Jane's Arkansas kitchen, Lauren loves to blend butter and sugar with family traditions to turn into delicious pastries. You will find the results of her work in our pastry case. Trained at the French Pastry School in Chicago, IL, Lauren worked at l'Etoile and Blackbird before running Batch Bakehouse.

Dan Mullins, Head Baker:

Baking bread is an art form. Dan enjoys the process, its multiple steps and required exactitude. He takes great joy in the simple steps of the delicate process. Dan came to Batch via New Orleans, where he worked for Emeril Lagasse.

Locally Owned and Operated:

Batch Bakehouse is owned and operated by two families, both of whom live under one mile from the bakery: Lauren Carter and her husband, Zachary Johnson; and Ian Gurfield and his wife Susan Detering. Lauren is the creative force behind Batch's pastry, Zach is a jack-of-all trades from delivery driver to bookkeeper. Ian (of Ian's Pizza) is the entrepreneurial mind, while Susan is a Jane-of-all trades, from design and marketing to sales. Batch is a certified Women-Owned business and proud member of the Greater Williamson Area Business Association.

Table Wine
Molly Moran

Have you ever found yourself wandering around a wine store trying to find a little gem that's interesting, delicious, and affordable?

At Table Wine, we curate a selection of wines that are exactly those cool finds that will excite you. Our customers know that if a wine is on our shelf, it's only because we believe in it wholeheartedly. We focus on wines for everyday occasions, meaning that the majority of our wines are under $20. We can point you towards wines that are perfect for parties, staples that should always be at your house, bottles that are worth splurging on, and everything in between. Bring us your menu for an upcoming dinner party and we'll happily find just the right drinks to beautifully complement your meal.

Our beer and spirit selection is just as carefully curated, and we pride ourselves on having the right amount of variety to keep you coming back.

One of the most rewarding parts of our job is introducing people to something new that they might not have tried and that they now love. We have a cozy bar inside our store, so people can enjoy a drink or two here. We want the world of wine to be fun and intriguing, and we offer wine classes and tastings for people who want to expand their horizons.

Located in the vibrant Schenk-Atwood neighborhood, Table Wine is a gathering spot for our community. We know our neighborhood well because we live and work here, and we want to create the store that's right for our neighbors. Table Wine is the neighborhood spot to pick up a bottle for tonight, have a drink with friends, or gather for one of our exciting events.

Machinery Row Bicycles
Christopher Quinn

Machinery Row Bicycles is located at the heart of downtown
Madison in the historic Machinery Row building. Based on the
shores of Lake Monona, the location provides an excellent
starting point for cycling enthusiasts and sightseers with
Madison's Capitol City Trail at our front door. The Machinery
Row building itself was designed in a commercial Romanesque
Revival Style by the architectural firm Conover and Porter,
giving it a castle-like appearance. The interior features exposed
brickwork and the wooden flooring of a century-old building
that has withstood the tests of time. Machinery Row Bicycles
boasts a large inventory of bicycles from manufacturers, such as
Trek, Giant, Felt, Co-Motion, Moots and Waterford.
Machinery Row rents bicycles as well, allowing visitors to enjoy
riding without bringing their own bicycles. Even wide-tired "fat
bikes" are part of the rental fleet, allowing adventurous cyclists
to explore the winter landscape. Clothing and accessories are
also in abundant supply ensuring visitors can obtain everything
they need for trips, whether long or short. The walls of the shop
are decorated with framed historic cycling posters produced
during the Victorian era, giving the visitor a glimpse of cycling
during that pioneering period. Original posters by Jean de
Paleologue are part of the permanent collection.

Madison and its surrounding communities are considered
among the most bike-friendly metropolitan areas in America,

boasting 186 miles of bike paths—paved and unpaved—that connect Dane County with the suburbs, downtown Madison, and the University of Wisconsin. In fact, Madison, has been considered a Platinum-level cycling community by the League of American Bicyclists since November, 2015. The Capitol City Trail and Southwest Commuter Trail are only a few of the many car-free paved paths that Madison has to offer. Bike lanes are also found throughout the city, covering 227 miles around Madison. With over 5% of Madison's citizens commuting or riding daily, cycling is a cultural centerpiece. The Madison B-Cycles bike share program has built 40 stations for users to rent a bike for a small fee when purchased on a smartphone app. Although the B-Cycles are only available from mid-March to mid-December, the stations have rented bicycles over 100,000 times during 2016 alone. Bike-friendly events such as the Midwest Bicycle Show and Sale, Concerts on the Square and Badger Football games have valet bike parking provided by the Wisconsin Bike Federation. The Red Bike Project pioneered by Budget Bicycle Center allows season-long rental of refurbished red-painted bicycles. The initial deposit is fully refundable at the end of the season and gives U.W. students the opportunity to use Madison's excellent bicycle infrastructure.

The landscape of Dane County has provided cyclists with a stunning backdrop for adventure. Madison's surrounding countryside features rolling hills that grow more challenging as riders approach Mount Horeb and Blue Mounds to the west. The IRONMAN Wisconsin bike course is found here, and is considered to be one of the top three most difficult in North America. Road races, such as the Spring Great Dane Velo Club criteriums and the Fast and Furious criterium add competition to the local calendar. In the fall, Cyclocross races make several stops in the Madison area. Parks in Verona, Sun Prairie, Fitchburg, and Madison are all stops on the Wisconsin Cyclocross calendar. Bring your cowbell and get ready to cheer racers from around the Midwest! Mountain bike single-track might be considered scarce in Dane County, but newcomers will find Cam-Rock Park in Cambridge, WI to be worth the drive.

Anthology
Laura & Sachi Komai

We grew up in Madison surrounded by many creative opportunities provided by public schools, the University of Wisconsin-Madison, community programs, and our parents. Drawing, painting, printing, quilting, collaging, photography, and many other forms of creative expression are an important part of our daily lives. However, it often seems that people don't have enough opportunities for creative expression, don't think of themselves as creative, or don't even know where to begin to explore their own talents and interests. The mission of our store is to facilitate creativity: to invite people to see the creativity in themselves and in the world around them. We believe strongly in the importance of creative expression for personal satisfaction and for the enrichment of our community. We opened Anthology in 2008 with a focus on providing a venue for the sale of works by local artists and indie crafters, including ourselves, providing space, information, and supplies for people to work on simple craft projects, and providing goods that spark our own creativity. As the store has grown, both of us have found more time to spend in the studio to design products for the store, many of which are produced by printers in the local area.

Our craft table at the back of the store has space for projects, such as card-making for Valentine's Day and Mother's Day. Our button machine is a popular attraction as many people enjoy bringing in their own images or writing/drawing their own designs and then pressing them into buttons. Over the years, we've become known for our Wisconsin-themed gifts, such as t-shirts, baby onesies, postcards, prints, pint glasses, tote bags, coasters, necklaces, and holiday ornaments.

bad dog frida
Sue Hunter

Located in a funky and charming little east side neighborhood, ten minutes from downtown Madison sits bad dog frida, a small store with a big heart. We sell dog and cat supplies, gifts, and give back to the neighborhood through fun in-store events, sales, and a great frequent buyer program. This little store is full of great products with locals in mind. Many of the foods and treats come from Wisconsin and all of the products in the store have been carefully selected to ensure quality with no edible ingredients from companies or countries with questionable practices. You can rest assured that your dog or cat will get a healthy and safe treat or food when you shop here.

This little store has the best customer service (for dogs and humans) you will find anywhere. People and dogs are greeted by name and treats are given to all the pooches that visit. It's like walking into a friendly local pub and finding friends who all know each other. Many a dog can be found outside the door after closing looking longingly into the store for just one more treat.

The neighborhood hosts some of the best restaurants in town; vegan, vegetarian, Lao, Thai, Tex-Mex, and the best chocolate shop in town featuring signature homemade dark chocolate truffles. Also, you can find many of the town's best local brew pubs right on Atwood Avenue. It's easy to see why this little shop does so well in this unique neighborhood. There is a bike path that winds right through Atwood Avenue and bikes are available for loan at a B-Cycle kiosk. Lake Monona is just a short walk (or ride) over from Atwood and a great place to rest after spending time shopping and eating.

The shop is clean, bright, fun, and full of color and life. You can select from the bulk treat options or bulk chews. Need help deciding what to get your particular dog? No worries— our staff is great at selecting the safest, longest lasting, good for a new puppy, and the tastiest chew or whatever it is you are looking for. Just ask and we are happy to help. If you need help fitting your dog into a harness or collar, we are ready to help with that, too. Our owners and staff know all our products and can help find something for any dog or cat who has allergies or sensitivities to certain ingredients. These are just some of the reasons why bad dog frida has been selected as one of the Best of Madison and Isthmus Favorites for many years running.

bad dog frida sells: treats, chews, toys, raw food, freeze dried, dehydrated foods, beds, leashes, collars and unique items such as car restraints, local dog ice cream, art work, and more for dogs and cats.

Hours of operation are: open seven days a week, Monday through Friday 10:00 am-7:00 p.m. and 9:00 a.m.-5:00 p.m. on Saturdays and Sundays. Located at 2094 Atwood Avenue, you can reach us by calling 608-442-6868. Parking is available behind the store or street parking is available as well.

The Knitting Tree
Jackie Shanahan

The Knitting Tree is my yarn, knitting supplies, jewelry and gifts retail shop in the trendy neighborhood of Monroe Street. The shop has been a fixture on this street since 1969.

I grew up around the corner on Commonwealth Street and I visited the original shop with my mother when I was a girl. Even at a young age I realized knitting was therapeutic and transformative because of its repetitive motions. And the tactile nature makes it a multi-sensory experience—serene and meditative. The colors and varieties of fibers fascinated me. Later, when my son was born, my interest in knitting was re-awakened and I began knitting with a vengeance, attempting more difficult patterns and projects. I began working at The Knitting Tree to support my love of knitting and bought the shop in 2006.

In 2014, we moved the shop two doors down and we are currently occupying the corner retail space of "The Monroe" building, on the corner of Monroe and Knickerbocker Streets. I was fortunate the new space in "The Monroe" building opened so close, so I could keep the store in the neighborhood. It was new and full of possibilities, yet virtually in the same location, being right next door. I have a photo stylist/set design background which served me well in creating my own space. We expanded our inventory to carry more jewelry, handbags, and ready-to-wear items, as well as quirky gift ideas.

It's a joy to come to work every day and offer such beautiful items to customers. I especially enjoy when someone finds just the right knitting project, the perfect bag to complement their lifestyle, wonderful jewelry to wear, or just a useful or unusual object. I know most of my customers by name and can remember their projects and the colors they chose. My brain just seems to work that way. It makes for a more delightful shopping experience for everyone.

I hope you feel the same when you stop to shop.

Mimosa
Ashley Leavy

Your New Age Resource Center: At Mimosa, we are dedicated to embrace the global diversity of wisdom and belief. We respect all integrity based teachings, systems, and spirit based philosophies. Our mission is to support and facilitate every individual's vision of what is meaningful to them in the spiritual realm. Without judgment or affiliation to one ideology, we embrace everyone's right to pursue their beliefs in a respectful and loving environment.

Mimosa also supports holistic, alternative healing paths, and the exploration of psychic and intuitive abilities. We cultivate an attitude of service toward each person as we help supply their needs. We take the time to get to know our customers and guide them in their choices of products, while creating a memorable and uplifting shopping experience.

Mimosa is one of State's Street's most unique stores. Our retail store features spiritual and metaphysical items from many different cultures and traditions. Mimosa has various in-house services, and participates as a vendor at local community festivals. We also maintain a resource list of spiritual and holistic practitioners in the area.

Mimosa opened its doors in May of 1984. The original owner, the late Patty Roth, had a vision of a community bookstore focused on the emerging alternatives in social thinking and beliefs. She also used the space for community programs. It was a very exciting time, and Madison owes Patty her deepest gratitude for her seventeen years of dedicated work to establish Mimosa as a key resource store for alternative choices.

Mimosa owes a great deal of gratitude to all of its various owners, past and present, who have each left their mark on this ever-evolving resource center.

In May of 2009, Mimosa was featured in the prestigious New Age Retailer Magazine as a highlighted thriving New Age business. Diane and Ashley were interviewed about their unique business insights and experiences. It was an honor to be included in this publication.

We are so very thankful for our knowledgeable, dedicated staff, without whom we couldn't be the Mimosa that we are today. Our sincere thanks go out to everyone, past and present, who has helped Mimosa along the way. We are grateful for all your hard work and the love that you have put into the store.

Wine and Hop Shop
Ben Feifarek

What's better than an ice-cold beer or a perfectly paired glass of wine? One that you made yourself!

The locally owned Wine and Hop Shop has been helping people make their own beer, wine, hard cider, and other fun fermentables, since 1972.

Do you want to brew beer but don't know where to start? The Shop has all the equipment you need to make your first batch, including starter kits with everything you need to brew beer at home.

Already a brewer and simply looking to make your next award-winning batch? The Shop offers more than 100 types of grain, hops, and yeast to make any kind of beer imaginable.

Is winemaking your thing? We've got fruit crushers, presses, fermenters, and ingredients to make all sorts of wine. Need a starter kit? Already have the fruit but just need yeast and other additives? Don't have fruit but want to make wine from concentrate? We've got you covered!

Everyone at the Wine and Hop Shop makes his or her own beer, wine, or other fermentables, so we're a passionate bunch who are ready to answer your questions. We make the experience interactive by offering classes, renting out equipment, and hosting contests. You can always bring in some beer or wine for us to taste, and we'll give you an honest assessment and suggestions for improvement.

And who knows, your new hobby could turn into a profession! The list of professional brewers and winemakers who got their start as patrons or employees of the Wine and Hop Shop is a long one and includes people working at Capital Brewery, One Barrel Brewing, Hop Haus, Lake Louie, House of Brews, Parched Eagle, Six Points Brewery, Pearl Street Brewery, Driftless Brewing, Wisconsin Brewing Company, MobCraft Brewing, Port Huron Brewing, Rockhound Brewery, Ale Asylum, Viking Brewpub, Lone Girl Brewing, Alt Brewing, Bent Kettle, Wollersheim Winery, King Fisher Winery, Bos Meadery, Cider House of Wisconsin, and Merchand's Cidery, among others.

You can find us seven days a week at 1919 Monroe Street, just up the street from the Camp Randall Stadium. Remember to enjoy a free sample of homemade beer, wine, or soda while you browse! Or, you can always find us online at wineandhop.com. We look forward to helping you start or hone your craft. Happy homebrewing!

Square Wine Company
Andrea Hillsey

Located on Madison's Capitol Square, Square Wine Company opened in the summer of 2012 to fill a void in the burgeoning farm-to-table scene. We wanted to be surrounded by many of the best restaurants in Madison that were pushing and guiding tastes in our city. We are dedicated to selling wines from small, family growers who make honest wines that reflect a sense of place. For us, wine is an extension of the dinner table.

Three philosophies drive the shop to this day and were also my reasons for opening. First and foremost, I want to sell wines that align with what Madisonians value in food. The farmers' market culture is very prominent here. People here care about how their food is sourced. We support importers, winemakers, and wines that are guided by sustainability—wines that may be farmed biodynamically, organically, or with a winemaker's personal approach. We want you to remember that wine is an agricultural product. The wines we sell are living and with that, they are always changing in the bottle. This is the magic of wine; we have seen how awesome and brilliant this idea is and believe it is our responsibility to share this great secret with you.

Secondly, we take great pride in hospitality. Our goal is to create a welcoming space where your experience is curated to your taste. Wine is intimidating enough. We like to think of ourselves as everyday sommeliers, helping you to get the most out of every wine drinking occasion.

Lastly, we like to take a more hands-on approach to retail. It's fun to help guide and educate consumers, but that can be really difficult without tastings. Tastings are crucial to education and also for helping a customer understand their preferences in wine. We offer weekly tastings at the shop every Friday night from 6:00-8:00pm ($20, $15 with RSVP) and every Saturday from 12:00-3:00pm ($10, waived with purchase). Won't you swing by?

Volunteer Opportunities

Literacy Network
Jeff Burkhart

You can discover Madison's rich cultural diversity while helping others to improve their lives. Literacy Network helps adults improve their reading, writing, and language skills. We serve nearly 1,200 people from 70 different countries, from Bhutan to Bolivia, from Madagascar to Mexico.

"I decided to get into this program because I wanted some education," said adult learner Aletta. "Because of the war in my country, I never had the opportunity to go to school."

One in seven adults faces literacy challenges every day in Dane County. That's 55,000 adults. That's enough to fill more than three Kohl Centers. Literacy is the key to access so much in our society, and is linked to every opportunity imaginable—better jobs, children's education, and access to health care.

Literacy Network is a thriving and growing organization. We are always looking for skilled volunteers and board members who can help move our mission forward. Volunteers drive our work. More than 900 volunteers gave nearly 30,000 hours of their time in 2016.

Thanks to the support of hundreds of donors and tutors, Literacy Network programs are in 28 different locations throughout Dane County, including public schools, libraries, hospitals, clinics, workplaces, community centers and a correctional facility.

Literacy Network collaborates with five school districts to offer our English in the schools' program, which helps parents better connect to their children's education. We do this because parents are a child's first and most important teacher. The single biggest factor in a child's educational success is the literacy level of his or her mother.

Five Madison libraries host our Skills in Computers and Literacy for Employment (SCALE) program to help adults build the individual computer skills they need to succeed in their careers. Several of our SCALE students find new and better employment after building their computer skills in class. With help from our staff and volunteers, Renee improved her computer skills, and after more than 20 years of unemployment, she got a job as a Captioning Assistant at CapTel. Renee got a second chance. "It feels good that society hasn't given up on you. Coming here has helped me feel like I could do something again," she said.

Nine local employers host programs to help their employees improve their on-the-job English skills. Several students have increased their hours, wages, and responsibility on the job.

St. Mary's Hospital and GHC host the collaborative English for Health program, which introduces adult learners to the complicated world of health care in the United States. Learners practice conversations with doctors, nurses, and pharmacists. They learn about healthy living and scheduling appointments. Myriam cut her cholesterol in half by eating better. Manuela made her own doctor's appointment and asked a pharmacist questions about a cold medicine. Juan Carlos found out how to access low-cost health insurance at a community health center after being laid-off and losing his job.

Because of hundreds of volunteers and donors, we are making great progress in helping people move forward in their lives. But there is so much more work to be done.

If you would like to learn more about how adult learners are overcoming literacy challenges, I invite you to call Literacy Network and learn more about getting involved. You can reach us at 608-244-3911.

Working Capital for Community Needs
Nancy Metzger

From Madison's Lake Mendota to Nicaragua's Lago de Managua, Working Capital for Community Needs (WCCN) has been building bridges between Madison, Wisconsin, and the working poor of Latin America for the past 30 years. WCCN empowers low-income Latin American entrepreneurs, women, and small-scale farmers through microcredit, fair trade, affordable housing projects, and women's empowerment initiatives. The primary program WCCN operates is The Capital for Communities Fund, a social investing fund channeling funds from socially responsible North American donors and investors to Latin American non-governmental organizations that specialize in providing credit and access to international markets for marginalized people. These efforts are at the source of providing better lives to women, indigenous people, and other historically marginalized communities.

Since 1984, WCCN—formerly the Wisconsin Coordinating Council on Nicaragua—has worked to establish healthy, equitable relations between the United States and Latin America, focusing first on Nicaragua due to the sister-state relationship between Wisconsin and Nicaragua under the Alliance for Progress, an initiative of John F. Kennedy. In 1991, WCCN helped develop the first private microfinance fund (called PrestaNic) in Nicaragua in collaboration with the

Council of Protestant Churches of Nicaragua (CEPAD) and subsequently with support from the Wisconsin Council of Churches. As WCCN grew in its resources, it was able to lend to additional non-parochial microfinance organizations.

In 2010, WCCN began providing value-chain financing to farmer's cooperatives, specifically to support access for coffee producers to fair-trade coffee markets, encouraging the growth of sustainable agricultural practices and food systems throughout the region. By providing short-term loans to coffee cooperatives at the time of harvest, WCCN can add to the 1.3 million farmers in more than 70 countries that are represented by the fair trade movement, ensuring more small-scale farmers are receiving a fair price for their coffee.

Today, WCCN aggregates citizen-investor financial resources in its Capital for Communities loan fund, and then offers these pooled resources in the form of reasonably priced loans to Latin America-based community development borrowers that ethically provide access to financial services, education, job opportunities, and other essential supportive social services to the working poor in their communities. The revenue generated from the borrowers' repayments are sufficient to pay back investors and cover basic operating expenses. WCCN reinvests earned surpluses back into its mission-driven programming.

WCCN now has partners in Ecuador, El Salvador, Honduras, Guatemala, Nicaragua, and Peru, and has invested over $110 million since 1991, providing a constant link over the past decades between Latin American micro-entrepreneurs and the impact investors of Wisconsin. These connections typically begin through financial ties, but take all sorts of shapes as they evolve. Through WCCN's efforts, opportunities for education, involvement in social change activism, and volunteer work in Latin America are available to all. These initiatives have been an essential part of a greater understanding of the inherently shared values of our fellow Americans, with whom we share much more than just a border.

To learn more about opportunities available to invest in, donate to, or visit WCCN's work in Latin America, visit their website, www.wccn.org.

Religion, Ethnicity, and Culture

Assumption Greek Orthodox Church

Visitors to Assumption Greek Orthodox Church, 11 North Seventh Street, may sense something beautiful in this urban church on Madison's east side. During the past seven decades, our members have included immigrants and natives from all parts of the world with diverse ethnic groups and races. Without their presence, the church would be an empty cavern. Through their faith in God and devotion to each other, the church is alive.

Assumption Greek Orthodox Church is a modern building with a spiritual ancestry of more than 2,000 years. Assumption Church and its sister Orthodox churches worldwide are in close spiritual union, even though the words of the prayers, hymns, and services are sung in many languages.

Beautiful vestments, music, incense, candle light processions, poetic words of praise, icons are brought together to worship God and celebrate creation. Since human beings possess both soul and body, the traditions practiced at Assumption Church offer both spiritual and physical gifts.

Assumption Church in Madison is part of the Metropolis of Chicago, composed of parishes in the states of Illinois, Wisconsin, Minnesota, Iowa, Missouri (except Kansas City), and several parishes in Indiana.

The first church at this site on the east side of Madison was Bashford Methodist Church built in the 1930s. In 1951, the Greek Orthodox community of Madison bought the building. An icon screen was installed and the church was transformed into a house of Eastern Christian worship.

The church in Madison, as in Eastern Christian churches worldwide, is divided into three general areas: the narthex, the nave, and the sanctuary.

In 1977, the building was re-designed by the late architect Alex Frunza, a member of the Assumption community and an immigrant from Romania. Frunza's design incorporated a portion of the original building and added the dome, sanctuary with apse, and transepts, which transformed the space into a traditional cruciform (cross-shaped) church. At that time, the church edifice was joined with an existing building for use as classrooms. During the 1990s, a marble floor was installed in the sanctuary and "solea" area near the icon screen.

A major addition and reconstruction project completed in 2016 added an elevator, which provides access to all three levels, new Sunday school rooms, an exo-narthex, office space, an expanded fellowship hall, and additional entrances.

The graceful arches and curved ceiling of the sanctuary combined with the cylindrical dome and overall cross shape make Assumption a modern, urban church, which remains true to Eastern Christian architectural traditions.

The adornment of Assumption Greek Orthodox Church with new, hand-painted icons by a member of the church community began in 1978 with the small portable icon of the Nativity of Jesus on the sanctuary wall over the Table of Oblation. The icon murals completed thus far cover approximately 2,400 square feet.

On the west wall of the church—the wall seen by people leaving the sanctuary—is an icon mural showing Mary, the mother of Jesus, as the central image, and a depiction of the Seventh Street neighborhood comprised of modest family homes. Mary is shown with her hands upraised in a gesture of prayer, or blessing, as an intercessor with God.

Mary's blessings are symbolized in the mural by thin lines or "rays" emanating near her hands toward a stylized depiction of Assumption Church and three houses reminiscent of the urban Madison neighborhood. The buildings are shown in reverse perspective, common to traditional icons.

While the stories that icons tell date back 2,000 years or more, modern stories are also included in the icon tradition of the church. Here in Madison, an icon of Saint Nectarios (died 1920) is shown on the south wall, which also bears icons of Saint Paul (1st century C.E.), Saint Anna, (the mother of Mary born in the pre-Christian era), and the Russian Saint Seraphim of Sarov (18th century).

Since the west wall of the nave is most visible while leaving the church, it is hoped the people leaving the sanctuary will transport the spiritual gifts they may have received inside the church to the streets outside and beyond.

Isthmus Zen Community
Ed Augustine

We live in turbulent and challenging times. Who are we? What is our purpose in living? Why is it that we cause so much pain for ourselves and for those with whom we share the planet? How do we cut through the delusion and hyperbole? When difficulties appear, how do we develop the presence and clarity to respond correctly?

Zen practice offers a way for each of us to understand this world and ourselves very deeply. We see the relationship we have with our mind. We see our daily clutter, our habitual patterns, our prejudices and beliefs and we see the subtle assumptions that run like background programming through our entire existence. We see our pain, anger, desire, and fear, and we engage with it all.

Zen is not about seeking some special state—some blissed-out or super-detached Samadhi. Zen is being fully engaged in your life just as it is right in front of you, right now. Each moment is complete just as it is. Engaged living, moment to moment, is an ever-continuing process, a process of penetration and digestion.

I once asked a student, "If understanding the true nature of your pain was the key to your enlightenment, how would that change the relationship?" Nothing demonstrates the working of the mind more clearly than those aspects we wish were not there. If something upsets you, look deeply into it. Where did it come from? What is it made of? What is the nature of your relationship with it? What does is cost you? What does it give? What *is* this? Look deeply into it and trust the wisdom of the moment.

Pleasure and pain, indeed all apparent opposites, arise as one. When we penetrate the moment, we see that all the opposites come together in one place right where we are sitting. We live in the place of synergy between all of these apparent opposites. There is no need to seek the middle way. We *are* the middle way. Opposition depends on our participation. As we begin to see this more clearly, we become increasingly less prone to being dragged around by our likes and dislikes. We learn to use our situation, everything that appears in it, and not to be used by it.

We are engaged. We participate. Our opposition softens, yet we know when it is useful and necessary. The teachings are no longer just words. The truth of it penetrates to the marrow. We become intimate with our lives, our hearts, our minds, and ourselves. And we also become intimate with the lives, hearts, and minds of those around us in an ever-increasing circle of concern. The opposition between self and other dissolves. It is then possible to respond with true wisdom and compassion to the situation in front of us right now, complete, just as it is.

Madison East Seventh-day Adventist Church
Hope Song

My journey with the Madison East Seventh-day Adventist Church began about 14 years ago when I received an invitation in the mail to a Bible prophecy seminar that spanned several weeks. My first inclination was to toss the handbill, but each time I picked it up to throw it out, the thought would come to me, "What would it hurt to go to just one?" And so I did go to one—each night, just one night at a time.

I searched out each Bible truth presented for myself, including the Seventh-Day Sabbath. God rested and blessed the seventh day and because there was first darkness, then light (Genesis 1:1-3), the Bible Sabbath is sundown Friday until sundown Saturday.

Adventist (Adventism) is the belief that Christ's second coming will soon occur. One reason for that belief comes from Daniel Chapter Two where a vision was given of the rise and fall of the four great monarchies, Babylon, Medo-Persia, Greece, and Rome and the God of heaven setting up His kingdom which shall stand forever. Matthew 24 and Luke 21 give signs to look for before Christ returns. "Immediately after the tribulation of those days (Christian persecution) shall the sun be darkened and the moon shall not give her light, and the stars shall fall from heaven." Christian persecution almost ceased about the middle of the 18th century, then, true to Christ's words, the signs of His coming at once began to appear. In history, May 19, 1780 is known as "the dark day" and November 13, 1833 as "the night the stars fell."

This journey has helped make sense of the chaos in the world as prophetic events continue to be fulfilled and my faith and personal relationship with God continue to strengthen with Bible study.

Our church offers classes on Sabbath morning for all ages, including children, to participate in and learn at their level.

Adventists also desire to minister to people's health needs by teaching healthy living classes and vegetarian cooking classes. Many enjoy fellowship together when we have a Sabbath vegetarian meal.

Our Pathfinders' Club and Adventurers' Club (similar to the scouts) are open to a wide range of ages and are another opportunity to participate. The Pathfinders and Adventurers are worldwide so many have met like-minded believers from all over the globe!

Do you like summer camps and retreats? There are teen camps and family camps in a beautiful nature setting for those who would like to be refreshed in nature. There are various men's, women's, young adult, and youth retreats all designed to meet the different needs of the people.

Our Christian school is right across the parking lot from the church and serves children up through 8th grade.

Are you searching for Bible truth in a warm and welcoming environment to give you certainty and hope?

People from many nations, kindreds, and tongues make up our loving church family. Please consider this an open invitation to join the journey! You are welcome to visit our Madison East Seventh-day Adventist Church! After all, what would it hurt to go (to church) just once?

Korean Presbyterian Church of Madison
eunuk Lim

The Korean Presbyterian Church of Madison (KPCM) was founded in March 21st, 1971. We are a church for Korean immigrants and Korean students studying in the University of Wisconsin. We are the first church to have worshiped in Korean in Madison. We joined PCUSA in 1980 and purchased the building in which we currently meet in 1994 where we've been worshipping since (6906 Colony Dr. Madison WI 53717).

As of 2017, we have about 130 people in our congregation, including Sunday school children.

Our Korean Presbyterian Church of Madison hopes to be a source of blessing in which God's grace is encountered, exchanged, and extended to the world. KPCM hopes to be a church that thinks of God's kingdom and raises Kingdom workers.

Mission Statement:

We strive to be a church that experiences:

God in worship

Family in small group

Joy in serving

Sunday worship

First Service (9:30 am): Highlights traditional worship (Choir)

Second Service (11:15 am): Highlights contemporary worship (Mahanaim worship team)

Small Group (Sarang bang)

Sarang bang refers to KPCM's small groups. It's a community where we share the "word" and "life" every Friday. There are five adult small groups and seven young adult small groups.

Serving:

We serve Christ's body, the church, according to the gifts and talents God has given each of us.

We strive to grow and mature the faith of the members through diverse training programs.

We welcome anyone who wishes to worship in Korean.

Madison Shambhala Center
Tuyet Cullen

Meditation has become the focus of much attention in our society. According to many research studies, meditation is worthy of this attention as its benefits are highly connected to increasing a person's health. The challenge is turning that attention into a habit that one incorporates into their life in order to see the health benefits. I have found this challenge to be invigorating, important, life-altering, heartfelt, and achingly beautiful. To support myself in this challenge, I made a careful decision to join the Madison Shambhala Center of Madison.

The Madison Shambhala Center of Madison is one of hundreds around the United States and the world that are part of Shambhala International. Succinctly, we offer meditation instruction. More expansively, we are a community of individuals who believe strongly in the goodness of individuals and society. Our mediation practice is a building block for putting our belief in goodness into action.

We offer many opportunities for members of the Madison community and beyond to experience goodness for themselves. Every Thursday, we offer a Weekly Dharma Gathering. All are welcome to attend. We have a half-hour of meditation with an option to receive meditation instruction. The half-hour is followed by a dharma talk given by one of our center's teachers. We also offer a time to socialize and chat with others from the center. This is a great introduction to our center and we invite you to attend.

We also offer public sitting hours: Mondays from 7:00 p.m. to 8:00 p.m. and Sundays from 9:00 a.m. to 11:00 a.m. These public sitting hours consist of sitting meditation and walking meditation. You are welcome to come and go as you please within the set time. Walking meditation tends to be on the half hour and we suggest arriving or leaving during that time.

During the public sit on the last Sunday of the month, we offer the Shambhala Sadhana, which is a way to generate and rejuvenate one's energy. An energy that is sent outward to society to express our belief in goodness.

For those who wish to have a deeper experience, we offer a wide variety of classes. These expand on topics that are shared at the Weekly Dharma Gathering with more opportunity for interaction and discussion. You can find a link to our website in my author bio.

We look forward to having you at our center.

American Hindu Association
Narend Reddy

American Hindu Association (AHA) Hindu Temple and Cultural Center, located at 2138 S. Fish Hatchery Road, Fitchburg on the western suburbs is a Hindu religious and cultural organization that serves the wider Madison community. AHA hosts seven acres of rural farmland property, which is a great place for the community to get out to and celebrate numerous indoor and outdoor festivals from early spring time through late fall. Here is a sample of some unique festivals that AHA organizes.

Colors & Kites Festival—May

The annual Color & Kites festival at AHA Hindu Temple and Cultural Center of Wisconsin mixes two traditional Hindu spring festivals—Makar Sankranti or Uttarayan (the kite festival), and Holi, also known as the festival of colors, where participants grab handfuls of colored powder and throw it into the sky to beats of popular music and rhythms.

Participants also put the colors all over their friends, family members, and sometimes even strangers. Additionally, there is live music, stalls for traditional Indian food and items, and lots of fun activities for kids.

Rathayatra & India Festival—June—July

AHA Hindu Temple celebrates the annual Jagannath Rathayatra and India Festival. This multi-cultural parade and festival is celebrated with live music, singing, classical dance, food stalls, stalls for traditional Indian items, and fun activities for kids.

The Ratha (*chariot*) Yatra (*festival*) is the oldest known parade in the world. It is a 5,000-year-old tradition of the celebration of Lord Krishna' return to Vrindaban. Millions of people from around the world descend on Puri, India to celebrate this unbelievable festival during the same time.

These outdoor festivals are a great way to wind down and relax in a celebratory way while mingling with community members and learning about unique traditions of India.

Other Hindu festivals, such as Krishna Janamasthmi, Ganesh Chaturthi (celebration of birthday of Lord Krishna and Lord Ganesha respectively), Dandiya folk dancing and the grand festival of Lights (Deepawali) are also celebrated in early fall. The AHA website has more detailed information on all the various community festivals and events that it hosts throughout the year.

All of these activities are designed to bring the community together, and are a chance for non-Hindus to participate and learn about the Hindu community as well. The events take place at Hindu Temple and Cultural Center of Wisconsin, 2138 South Fish Hatchery Road. There is usually no entry fee or very minimal charge to cover event expenses.

AHA is also in the final stages of building a fully-fledged Temple and Cultural Center facility and also has a resident priest at the temple for the benefit of the devotees and the community. This makes it a great place to drop by and learn about the Hindu religion, traditions, and culture.

AHA is a non-profit organization run fully by community volunteers who have settled in Madison from various parts of the world. All members of the Madison community are welcome at AHA events, with the only criteria being the participants respect the mission, vision, and the guiding principles of vegetarianism and non-alcoholic beverage consumption while on AHA property.

More information on the AHA events, programs, and the organization can be found on our website and Facebook page.

Cambrian Heritage Society of Madison, Wisconsin
Danny Proud

If you are proud of your Irish or Scottish heritage, with those Celtic roots, then you are lucky. Everyone knows about bagpipes, kilts, Highland dancing, and tall tales and music sessions in Irish pubs. As for me, I grew up knowing precious little about my roots from another Celtic group, the Welsh. I wanted to find out more about where my father's family came from, to find a heritage I could connect with.

One day, I found out about a Welsh festival in town, so I joined my parents and went to a few events over a Labor Day weekend. That weekend changed my life.

There, in the company of hundreds of Welsh-Americans, I was given a peek at who the Welsh are and what is important to them. I was blown away by the power and beauty of the community singing. I loved the camaraderie of the people, their cheerful manner, and their love of history and the arts. I wanted to find out more about this wonderful new world that was opening up to me.

I started attending the local Welsh society that offered language lessons and social events, always with music. I learned a bit of the Cymraeg language so I could sing the songs. I played guitar and sang in a folk band that sprang up.

Joining the Cambrian Heritage Society of Madison has given me the chance to meet people with a shared heritage, and a shared love of the things that Wales is known for. I am now taking harp lessons, go to a language camp for a week every summer, and attend singing festivals all over Wisconsin. At society meetings in Madison, I listen to presentations on historical accounts spanning centuries in Britain as well as to stories from the early years of settlers coming to Wisconsin. In Madison we have hosted the Bangor Male Voice Choir from Wales and artists such as Robin Huw Bowen, the triple harpist.

My life is enriched through my involvement in Welsh-American organizations, such as the Cambrian Heritage Society. I have grown in the areas of music and language and literature, and have become a rugby fan. I have a deepening interest in the history of Wisconsin and the U.S. and a greater appreciation for other ethnic groups whose stories of coming to America are so similar. I have connected with many other Wales enthusiasts who have so much to share. In turn, I offer the music and language for others to listen to and learn from, much to their delight. I now have a sense of grounding, of knowing where I come from.

About Z Publishing

Having begun as a blog in the fall of 2015, Z Publishing, LLC is currently transitioning into book publishing. This transition is in response to the problem plaguing the publishing world: For writers, finding new readers can be tremendously difficult, and for readers, finding new, talented authors with whom they identify is like finding a needle in a haystack. With Z Publishing, no longer will anyone have to go about this process alone. By producing anthologies of multiple authors rather than single-author volumes, Z Publishing hopes to harbor a community of readers and writers, bringing all sides of the industry closer together.

To sign up for the Z Publishing newsletter or to submit your own writing to a future anthology, visit www.zpublishinghouse.com.

You can also follow the evolution of Z Publishing on the following platforms:

Facebook: www.facebook.com/zpublishing

Twitter: www.twitter.com/z_publishing

Author Biographies
(In Order of Appearance)

MUSEUMS

James Lattis: Doctor James Lattis is the Director of UW Space Place and Faculty Associate in the Department of Astronomy of the University of Wisconsin-Madison. He is also a historian of astronomy. For more about UW Space Place and Planet Trek Dane County, see http://spaceplace.wisc.edu. For more about the UW-Madison Astronomy Department, see http://www.astro.wisc.edu. For more on Washburn Observatory, see http://go.wisc.edu/washobs. For more on the history of astronomy at UW-Madison and in Wisconsin, see http://go.wisc.edu/washobshistory.

March Schweitzer: March Schweitzer moved to Madison from Washington D.C. 35 years ago. She is the owner/operator of Madison City Tours, which offers private city and Frank Lloyd Wright sightseeing tours by van as well as step-on guide services. March serves on the boards of Historic Madison and Friends of the Meeting House, a Frank Lloyd Wright National Historic Landmark. She recently authored a booklet entitled, "That's Wright! A Self-Guided, Driving Tour of Wright's Life and Works in Madison," which is available from her tour website, madisoncitytours.com.

Ann Waidelich: Ann Waidelich is a retired librarian, Madison historian, and curator of the historic Nathaniel & Harriet Dean House run by the Historic Blooming Grove Historical Society.

Arianna Murphy: Arianna Murphy is the Executive Director of the Wisconsin Science Museum and has been working in the museum profession for eight years. Born in Beloit, Arianna is proud to call Wisconsin her home. As the founding director of the museum, she is passionate about fostering an experiential hands-on environment where visitors can freely and safely explore ideas and have conversations.

OUTDOORS

Mike Gaspard: Mike Gaspard, General Manager at University Ridge, has been with the UW Athletic Department since 2009, and served the previous year under the management of Palmer Golf. Gaspard oversees all aspects of golf and cross country skiing at the University Ridge property. Prior to coming to Wisconsin, Gaspard previously served as the Tournament Coordinator (2002-2003) and as Head Golf Professional (2004-2007) at JW Marriott Wildfire Golf Club in Phoenix, Arizona. Gaspard also served as an Assistant Golf Professional at the Westin Kierland Resort & Spa in Scottsdale, AZ from 2000-2002. Gaspard earned a B.S. in Retail Management from UW Madison in 2000. He completed the PGA PGM program in 2006, and was honored with the Acushnet Scholarship. Gaspard was the 2009 recipient of the

Wisconsin PGA Merchandiser of the Year. A native of Waukesha, Wis., Gaspard resides in Madison with his wife Julene, son Garryck, and daughter Graciela.

Mills Botham: Mills Botham is the 2016-2017 Commodore (President) of the Hoofer Sailing Club in Madison Wisconsin. A Madison native, Mills grew up sailing on Lake Mendota in the Hoofer Youth program, and later became an instructor in the same program, teaching in the summers between his sophomore, junior, and senior years at West High School. He is now a sophomore at UW Madison majoring in History, and continues to teach sailing in the summer. He was elected Commodore of the Hoofer Sailing Club in August of 2016. Mills' time with the Hoofer Sailing Club has shaped a great deal of his identity, and he is proud to be a part of it. He can be reached at <u>commodore@hoofersailing.org.</u>

Aldo Leopold Nature Center: The Aldo Leopold Nature Center (ALNC) was established in 1994 as an independent, non-profit organization with the mission of engaging and educating current and future generations, empowering them to respect, protect, and enjoy the natural world. For more information about our programs and facilities or to learn how you can get involved, please contact the Aldo Leopold Nature Center (608-221-0404) or visit us online at <u>www.aldoleopoldnaturecenter.org.</u>

Ryan Brinza: Ryan Brinza is the PGA Head Golf Professional with the City of Madison Golf Courses. He grew up just outside of Madison and has worked in golf for the past 17 years in and around Madison. Ryan enjoys the history of the City of Madison Golf Courses just as much as he enjoys playing on them.

ART & LITERATURE

KelsyAnne Schoenhaar: As Encore's founding artistic director and resident playwright, Kelsy began her tenure at Encore in May of 2000. Kelsy has a diverse educational background, including a full scholarship to the Northern Illinois University School of Music, and two business degrees including an MBA from Cal Southern University (summa cum laude). With many years of experience managing human service programs in the Chicago area and working as a professional musician (began professional career at age 12) and as a producing and directing playwright, Kelsy has taken her varied experiences and her vision of what a professional theater for people with disabilities should look like and put it to work for Encore. As a composer, and a musician who is proficient in playing more than 30 instruments, a filmmaker, and a nationally published photographer, Kelsy offers diversity equal to the range of the stories told and the talents of the Encore actors and staff.

Paula Panczenko: Paula Panczenko joined the UW-Madison's Tandem Press in 1989 and is responsible for planning and implementing Tandem's artistic and administrative policies. Tandem Press is now recognized as one of the leading fine art presses in the United States and exhibits its prints in New York, Chicago, and Miami annually. She currently serves as President of the International Fine Print Dealers Association. For more information on Tandem Press, please visit www.tandempress.wisc.edu, or contact the Tandem Press team via phone (608-263-3437) or email (info@tandempress.wisc.edu).

Shana Verstegen: Co-owner of Madison Log Rolling, Shana has been involved in log rolling since 1987. She holds many amateur, semi-professional, and professional log rolling titles, and is a four-time log rolling and two-time boom running WORLD champion. She is a Great Outdoor Games and ESPN STIHL Timbersports Series Gold Medalist. A graduate of UW with a major in Kinesiology, she is the fitness director at Supreme Health and Fitness in Madison, WI, and a Master Instructor for the American Council on Exercise and TRX. For more info visit: http://www.shanaverstegen.com

Olivia Judd: Co-owner of Madison Log Rolling, Olivia has been log rolling since 1998. She holds many amateur titles including amateur world champion, and is a semi-pro world champion. Olivia has appeared on ESPN and ESPN2, competing in the Great Outdoor Games and in the STIHL Timbersports Series Boom Run event. She has co-taught the Madison Logrolling program with Shana since 2005. Olivia is a student at the University of Minnesota Law School.

Samantha B. Crownover: Samantha Crownover is a leader in the Madison arts community. She is the Executive Director of Bach Dancing & Dynamite Society, a summer chamber music festival. She is also board president of Wormfarm Institute, where culture and agriculture meet on the

146

urban/rural continuum. Samantha is involved in many arts and architecture-based projects, ranging from managing events for Performing the Jewish Archive to consulting on collection managements and caring for historic buildings. She served as curator of Tandem Press, a fine-art studio at UW-Madison, and has served as board president of the Madison Trust for Historic Preservation and as the Friends board president of the UW-Madison Geology Museum. Visit bachdancinganddynamite.org.

Kari Fisher: Kari is the Artistic Director and owner of "Synergy Dance Academy." She received her dance training at Monona Academy of Dance under the direction of Jo Jean Retrum and Jean Adams. She took classes in tap, jazz, and ballet for 12 years and was a part of the Wisconsin Dance Ensemble's Nutcraker for 10 years. Kari brings over 15 years of experience as an educator, artist, and community volunteer. She has an Associate Degree in Commercial Art from Madison Area Technical College and a Bachelor of Science Degree in Elementary Education from Edgewood College. Kari has lived in the Madison area her whole life and has strong ties to the community through her various volunteer/leadership positions which include being Past President of the Junior League of Madison. Kari has been involved with various local organizations including The Ronald McDonald House, The Madison's Children's Museum, AGrace Hospice Care, Girl Scouts of America, Habitat for Humanity, Leadership Greater Madison, Edgewood Campus School, Fishing Without Boundaries, Special Olympics, American Family Children's Hospital, and the Susan B. Koman Foundation. Kari has been the owner of Something Fishy for 13 years, through which she has produced various art pieces, from murals to mosaics. Her mosaic cow brought the highest auctioned price of the 2006 Madison Cows on Parade benefitting the American Family's Children's Hospital. Her cow is on display at the UW School of Nursing. Another mosaic piece of hers, "Fleming the Flamingo," was created to benefit Henry Vilas Zoo. Kari's enthusiasm for dance education as well as her organizational and leadership skills is something she is excited to share with the parents, students, and staff of Synergy Dance Academy.

Jennifer A. Lapham & Brian Kluge: Owner and founder of Midwest Clay Project, Jennifer A. Lapham brings over 20 years of experience as an artist and educator to the studio. Lapham decided to pursue her interest in ceramics shortly after receiving a BA (1988) in Liberal Arts from St. John's College, Annapolis, MD, and completing two years of post-baccalaureate studies (1993) at the New York State College of Ceramics at Alfred University in Alfred, NY. She received her MFA (1996) in ceramics from the School of the Art Institute of Chicago and began an 11-year stretch teaching in academia. In addition to her work as an educator, Lapham exhibited her artwork nationally from 1996-2007, which included collaborative projects with her partner Paul Sacaridiz. Brian Kluge is an artist whose studio practice is rooted primarily in ceramics. He earned a Bachelor of Science in Art Education from the UW-Madison and a Master of Fine Arts from the University of Nebraska-Lincoln. Kluge was named an emerging talent in Ceramics Monthly in 2012 and has completed artist residencies at the LUX Center for the Arts and the Roswell Artist-in-Residence Program. He exhibits his sculptures nationally and teaches art in a variety of capacities to people of all ages. He currently teaches ceramics at Madison College and the University of Wisconsin-Madison and runs the

Midwest Clay Project. Visit www.briankluge.com for more information. For inquiries: Midwest Clay Project 2040 Winnebago Street Madison, WI 53704 (608) 255-9240 info@midwestclayproject.com www.midwestclayproject.com.

Denny Berkery: Denny Berkery is the owner of The Vinery. After 34 years, he still maintains his passion for art glass. His focus on education has been a prominent part of his business. Berkery is a mentor to many stained glass artists, retailers, and educators. He is a director of the KBW Foundation, a nonprofit organization that promotes art glass in schools. Developing curriculum and providing scholarships are a few of the efforts of this organization. Becoming involved with the schools as an artist in residence has been one of his favorite activities. Engaging children in the process of creating with mosaics and fused glass has been most rewarding. Being surrounded by staff who share his passion makes The Vinery a truly special place to experience.

Esty Dinur: Esty Dinur's writing has been published in numerous local, national, and international publications. See some of her articles here: http://isthmus.com/topics/esty-dinur/ She is the host of a weekly call-in show on WORT, 89.9 FM, www.wortfm.org and works as the Communications, Community Relations, and Publicity Director of the Wisconsin Union Theater.

HEALTH & FITNESS

Arielle Juliette: A professional dancer since 2006, Arielle

Juliette is the owner of Dance Life and gladly dedicates her time and energy to upholding the Dance Life philosophies of fun, wellness, and community. Arielle would love to hear from you about what you read here, so please send her a message at info@madisondancelife.com, or head over to the Dance Life website to see more about her classes and events at www.madisondancelife.com.

Jennifer Crye: Jennifer Crye, LMT, has been a licensed massage therapist in Wisconsin since 2000. She is also an ACE Certified personal trainer. She has been the Volunteer Massage Captain at the Ironman Wisconsin in Madison, WI for the last 15 years. She is always striving to help people live a healthy lifestyle through exercise, diet, and massage. She enjoys running, biking, hiking, kayaking, skiing, and all the outdoor activities that Wisconsin has to offer. You can visit www.yourbodyharmony.com to find out more about Body Harmony and its therapists and to schedule an appointment.

Greg Griffin: Greg Griffin is the owner-operator at Float Madison, Madison's downtown float therapy center. He has been involved in the wellness industry since 2008 after having his own personal health crisis, and he has made it his mission to provide Madison and the surrounding areas with a premium float therapy experience. Greg has done most of the start-up and operating work himself, including marketing, painting, interior design, web design and running the studio every second they are open, which shows how much he cares about providing an awesome float experience for his community. To learn more about Greg and Float Madison, visit floatmadison.com.

Kara Donovan-Guido: Kara Donovan-Guido, LMT Lighthouse Healing Massage Therapy, LLC 6441 Enterprise Lane Suite 212B Madison, WI 53719 www.lighthousehealing.com, (608) 216-6761.

Vanessa and Alla: Vanessa and Alla came together with a common vision of helping the community have a deeper knowledge of health and well-being. Both certified herbalists began teaching kombucha classes in 2005 together in Madison. They soon became well known for their kombucha knowledge and word of their expertise spread. Workshops sold out and they soon had a SCOBY farm growing! They decided to work together to create one of the nation's first small local kombucha businesses. Alla and Vanessa can often be seen talking excitedly about new business growth and random silly things. You will find them if you just follow the loud laughter that is carried by the wind, and if you happen to engage in conversation, don't be surprised if they both answer you at the same time in stereo! Alla and Vanessa consider themselves non-sexual soul mates and believe that they were put here together to create something powerful and wonderful. Cheers! Nas da Rovia! (to your health).

FUN

Nathan Greenawalt: Nathan Greenawalt founded and runs the Old Sugar Distillery. He is a graduate of UW-Madison. He loves to sail, bicycle, hang out with his children, and make creative cocktails for his friends and family.

Darwin Sampson: Darwin Sampson is a 47-year old owner and operator of The Frequency in Madison WI (eight years). He was born and raised in Fond du Lac, WI and has been a Madison resident since 1996.

Maureen C. Easton: Maureen C. Easton is the owner of ALT Brew.

Lauren Glover: Lauren Glover is a Doctoral Candidate at UW-Madison School of Archaeology and Anthropology. She writes fan fiction and fantasy stories. She is part owner of Cat Cafe Mad with her mother Cheryl and brother Kirk.

Scott Haden: Scott Haden manages the marketing and advertising life of Forward Theater. He returned to Madison after serving as Managing Director of the Rocky Mountain Repertory Theatre for the last three years. Scott has also enjoyed acting for various regional theatres across the country, including the Utah Shakespeare Festival, Chicago Shakespeare Theatre, Writers' Theatre (Jeff Nomination), Madison Repertory Theatre, Milwaukee Chamber Theatre, Theatre at the Center and the American Players Theatre. He is a proud member of Actors' Equity, and a founding member of the Wisconsin Story Project, the Dolphinback Theatre, and the Lovewell Theatre Project, an ensemble of artists that conceive and compose original musicals during intensive three-week collaborations. Scott holds a BFA in Acting from the Webster University Conservatory of Theatre Arts in St. Louis.

Brittany Hammer: Brittany Hammer graduated from the University of Wisconsin-Stout with a degree in Hotel,

Restaurant, and Tourism Management. Upon graduating, Brittany worked as a restaurant manager in Minneapolis and Madison. She always had the dream of running her own business, thinking it would be a restaurant, but after taking a food tour, she realized this was the perfect experience for her to bring people happiness through food and hospitality. Feel free to visit Capital City Food Tours website at www.capitalcityfoodtours.com or contact Brittany with any questions at brittany@capitalcityfoodtours.com.

Jacci Meier: Jacci Meier serves on the Mad-City Board of Directors as Corresponding Secretary. Her family has been a part of the ski team since 2003.

Aaron Bakken: Aaron Bakken is co-owner of Rockin' Jump parks in Madison, WI, and Eagan, MN. He was the first person hired by the founders of Rockin' Jump when the company was founded in 2010, charged with developing their brand. Since then he held roles as their Director of Marketing, Franchise Sales Director, and is now enjoying the role of a multi-unit franchise owner. Prior to joining Rockin' Jump, Aaron founded six small companies, including a branding and graphic design agency, a day spa / retail business, an online retail company, an online student debt consolidation consultancy, and an international import/export consultancy. Suffice it to say, the role as a trampoline and indoor activity park owner has been the most fun endeavor he's taken on so far.

Chef Joel Olson: Chef Joel Olson of Hemmachef (www.Hemmachef.com) is a nationally-recognized culinary instructor for children, youth, and adults with over 20 years of teaching experience. He has taught cooking skills and manners and etiquette to individuals of all levels of ability, interest, and experience, including those with special needs. He has taught across the nation and has founded a culinary education program, toured as a celebrity chef, volunteered in after-school cooking and anti-hunger programs, conducted summer cooking camps, run numerous culinary events, and started his own business. Chef Joel has been a pastry chef, private chef, personal chef, caterer, restaurant chef, food writer, and television and radio chef, as well as a culinary instructor. He is experienced in leading large and small groups and is available for events ranging from corporate team-building, professional bonding events, and culinary presentations to children's birthday parties and in-home dinner parties.

Tania Tandias: Tania Tandias has studied flamenco and Spanish classical dance with top dancers in the United States and Spain, including Pablo Rodarte, Eva Enciñias-Sandoval, Rosa Montoya, Juana Amaya, and numerous other Spanish artists. Ms. Tandias has performed with Alma Flamenca in Albuquerque and with Maria Benitez's Nuevo Flamenco in Santa Fe. She has also recently choreographed and performed in pieces for the Madison Opera, Bach Dancing and Dynamite Society, Milwaukee Ballet, Kanopy Dance Company, Oshkosh Symphony Orchestra and the Wisconsin Chamber Orchestra. In 2016, Ms. Tandias was honored to receive the "Performance/Choreography Award" from the Wisconsin Dance Council. Tania Tandias now lives in her hometown of Madison where she teaches, performs, and directs her company Tania Tandias Flamenco & Spanish Dance. For more information, contact Tania at tandias@usa.net or visit www.flamencodance.net.

Nancy McClements: Nancy McClements came to Scottish Country Dancing in 1983 after a semester of ballet found her wanting a more social and energetic activity. She is the Chair of Madison Scottish Country Dancers, and has her preliminary teaching certificate from the Royal Scottish Country Dance Society. She would rather dance than teach! You can contact her at nancymcclements@gmail.com. Learn more about MSCD at madisonscottishcountrydancers.org or at https://www.facebook.com/scottishdancemadison/.

Joshua Perkins: Josh Perkins has been writing and publishing on a variety of topics, traditional music being one, since he was 12. Now mainly a food writer as part of his job as chef for K-12 food programs, he makes his home with his family in Madison, actively pursuing his hobbies of playing Irish and Scottish music and making wood-fired pizza.

Justin Schmitz: Justin Schmitz is co-owner and CEO of Hop Head Tours. Originally form Appleton, WI, he studied Recreation and Business Administration at Western State College of Colorado working as a whitewater rafting and kayaking guide in the summers and a bartender at a local brewery and a mountain resort during the winters. Justin combines his love of travel, recreation, and craft beer into a lifestyle and a business. Feel free to contact him at Justin@hopheadtours.com.

SHOPS

Staci Fritz: Staci Fritz is a co-owner of Calliope Ice Cream. Originally from Iowa, she lived in the San Francisco Bay Area for almost 20 years. After getting a degree in Graphic Design and working in copywriting, marketing, and management, she ultimately decided that Wisconsin was where she needed to be. If you would like to learn more about Calliope, or talk about Madison, small business ownership, or food-based entrepreneurial endeavors, she can be reached at staci@calliopeicecream.com.

Molly Moran: Molly Moran is the owner of Table Wine in Madison. She worked in restaurants and in the beverage industry for years before opening her own wine/beer/spirits store in December 2015. To see what's happening at the store, visit our website: www.tablewinemadison.com.

Christopher Quinn: Christopher Quinn is a Wisconsin native and a graduate of the University of Wisconsin-Green Bay with a Bachelor of Science degree. He has worked in the bicycle industry in sales, store management, website content management, custom bicycle fitting and as a bike tour mechanic. He is a lifetime cyclist and competes in Masters' Cyclocross racing every fall.

Laura & Sachi Komai: Laura and Sachi Komai have lived in Madison for most of their lives. Laura earned her B.A. in Geology from Gustavus Adolphus College in St. Peter, Minnesota and Sachi earned her B.A. in English and Art from Cornell College in Mt. Vernon, Iowa. Both sisters returned to Madison for graduate study at the UW-Madison; Laura earning an M.S. in Geography and Sachi earning an M.F.A in Graphics. They first worked together as co-managers of a local gift store before deciding to add more creativity to their retail careers, opening Anthology in 2008. You can follow Anthology on Facebook and Instagram at Anthology218.

Jackie Shanahan: Jackie Shanahan is the proprietor of The Knitting Tree in Madison, Wisconsin. She is a renowned expert knitter, knitwear designer, and shop owner.

Ben Feifarek: Ben Feifarek began home brewing in 2003 when he helped a buddy brew a Pete's Wicked Ale clone recipe. He was hooked from the first brew. Soon after, Ben started his own Beer of the Month club, where he brewed four batches of beer a month and published an accompanying magazine filled with articles, stories, and games centered on beer. The Club had around 15 members who each enjoyed a six-pack of experimental beer each month. During this beer brewing frenzy, Ben visited his local homebrew shop, the Wine and Hop Shop, and applied for a job. And the rest, as they say, is history.

Andrea Hillsey: Andrea Hillsey is the owner/operator of Square Wine Co. Originally from Michigan, Andrea played softball at Purdue University and then headed to Miami, FL to study hospitality at Florida International University. It was during this time when she learned there was more to wine than just juice in a glass. She is a Certified Sommelier through the International Sommelier Guild. When she is not slinging wine, you'll find her squeezing dogs or on her bike.

VOLUNTEER OPPORTUNITIES

Jeff Burkhart: Jeff Burkhart is the Executive Director of Literacy Network of Dane County, a not-for-profit organization serving adults and families. He holds an M.S. in Continuing and Vocational Education from University of Wisconsin-Madison and a B.A. in Journalism from Indiana University. Jeff brings 20 years of program development in the field of adult literacy. In his time at Literacy Network, the organization has created nationally recognized programs, expanded programming to 28 locations throughout Dane County, developed numerous partnerships to support adults and families, and moved into a new custom-designed learning center in South Madison in September 2016.

Nancy Metzger: Prior to joining WCCN, Nancy was the Financial Service Practice Leader and Associate Vice President for the International Executive Service Corps (IESC). With more than 15 years of private sector development and international management experience, she brings practical knowledge and technical expertise in financial services, commercial law, corporate governance, non-bank financial institutions (fund) development, and proposal writing. She also has in-depth organizational development experience. Nancy joined IESC from SNV, the Netherlands Development Organization, where she served as Deputy Regional Director for Latin America from 2009-2011. Prior to SNV, Nancy was Senior Project Officer in the Capital Markets and Corporate Governance Department at the International Finance Corporation of the World Bank Group in charge of Latin American program-related investments on behalf of a donor trust fund.

RELIGION, ETHNICITY, AND CULTURE
158

Ed Augustine: Ed Augustine, Abbot, Isthmus Zen Community Ed is a Senior Dharma Teacher with the Kwan Um School of Zen and has been practicing within the Kwan Um School for 15 years. Ed is a musician, composer, outdoor enthusiast, and is curious about everything in the universe. He has made a study of philosophy, history, science, music, religion, spirituality and meditation for nearly 40 years. Visit isthmuszencommunity.org, kwanumzen.org for more information.

Hope Song: Hope Song is a member of the Madison East Seventh-day Adventist Church in Madison, WI. Originally from Wisconsin, Hope enjoys family, studying the Bible, and gardening. It truly is a marvel to see how God's ways are higher than our ways! Please visit the church's website to learn more about our church or join us for worship: www.madisonadventistchurch.com.

Eunuk Lim: Eunuk Lim is the pastor of Korean Presbyterian Church of Madison.

Tuyet Cullen: Tuyet Cullen is the Center Director of the Madison Shambhala Center (www.madison.shambhala.org). She is committed to creating the ground for the principles of Basic Goodness to flourish. She believes her path as a meditator is one and the same as her path as a woman of color.

Narend Reddy: Narend is the President of Board of Directors for American Hindu Association in Madison.

Danny Proud. Danny Proud is a board member of the Cambrian Heritage Society in Madison. He regularly presents programs or performances on Welsh music, language, or culture at festivals, courses, and other events.

Made in the USA
Lexington, KY
01 June 2019